THE WAY PEOPLE LIVE

Life in Ancient Athens

Titles in The Way People Live series include:

THE WAY PEOPLE LIVE

Life in Ancient Athens

by Don Nardo

Lucent Books, P.O. Box 289011, San Diego, CA 92198-9011

Library of Congress Cataloging-in-Publication Data

Nardo, Don, 1947–
    Life in ancient Athens / by Don Nardo.
        p.   cm. — (The way people live)
    Includes bibliographical references and index.
    Summary: Discusses life in ancient Athens, including the growth of the
city-state and its government, religious beliefs, festivals, customs, athletic
games and sports, the visual arts, and the involvement of Athens in war on
land and sea.
    ISBN 1-56006-494-3 (lib. bdg.)
    1. Athens (Greece)—Civilization Juvenile literature.   2. Greeks—Social
life and customs Juvenile literature.   [1. Athens (Greece)—Civilization.
2. Greece—Civilization—To 146 B.C.]   I. Title.   II. Series.
DF275.N37   2000
938'.5—dc21   99-24576
                                                                                    CIP

Contents

Discovering the Humanity in Us All

Books in The Way People Live series focus on groups of people in a wide variety of circumstances, settings, and time periods. Some books focus on different cultural groups, others, on people in a particular historical time period, while others cover people involved in a specific event. Each book emphasizes the daily routines, personal and historical struggles, and achievements of people from all walks of life.

To really understand any culture, it is necessary to strip the mind of the common notions we hold about groups of people. These stereotypes are the archenemies of learning. It does not even matter whether the stereotypes are positive or negative; they are confining and tight. Removing them is a challenge that's not easily met, as anyone who has ever tried it will admit. Ideas that do not fit into the templates we create are unwelcome visitors—ones we would prefer remain quietly in a corner or forgotten room.

The cowboy of the Old West is a good example of such confining roles. The cowboy was courageous, yet soft-spoken. His time (it is always a he, in our template) was spent alternatively saving a rancher's daughter from certain death on a runaway stagecoach, or shooting it out with rustlers. At times, of course, he was likely to get a little crazy in town after a trail drive, but for the most part, he was the epitome of inner strength. It is disconcerting to find out that the cowboy is human, even a bit childish. Can it really be true that cowboys would line up to help the cook on the trail drive grind coffee, just hoping he would give them a little stick of peppermint candy that came with the coffee shipment? The idea of tough cowboys vying with one another to help "Coosie" (as they called their cooks) for a bit of candy seems silly and out of place.

So is the vision of Eskimos playing video games and watching MTV, living in prefab housing in the Arctic. It just does not fit with what "Eskimo" means. We are far more comfortable with snow igloos and whale blubber, harpoons and kayaks.

Although the cultures dealt with in Lucent's The Way People Live series are often historically and socially well known, the emphasis is on the personal aspects of life. Groups of people, while unquestionably affected by their politics and their governmental structures, are more than those institutions. How do people in a particular time and place educate their children? What do they eat? And how do they build their houses? What kinds of work do they do? What kinds of games do they enjoy? The answers to these questions bring these cultures to life. People's lives are revealed in the particulars and only by knowing the particulars can we understand these cultures' will to survive and their moments of weakness and greatness.

This is not to say that understanding politics does not help to understand a culture. There is no question that the Warsaw ghetto, for example, was a culture that was brought about by the politics and social ideas of Adolf

Hitler and the Third Reich. But the Jews who were crowded together in the ghetto cannot be understood by the Reich's politics. Their life was a day-to-day battle for existence, and the creativity and methods they used to prolong their lives is a vital story of human perseverance that would be denied by focusing only on the institutions of Hitler's Germany. Knowing that children as young as five or six outwitted Nazi guards on a daily basis, that Jewish policemen helped the Germans control the ghetto, that children attended secret schools in the ghetto and even earned diplomas—these are the things that reveal the fabric of life, that can inspire, intrigue, and amaze.

Books in The Way People Live series allow both the casual reader and the student to see humans as victims, heroes, and onlookers. And although humans act in ways that can fill us with feelings of sorrow and revulsion, it is important to remember that "hero," "predator," and "victim" are dangerous terms. Heaping undue pity or praise on people reduces them to objects, and strips them of their humanity.

Seeing the Jews of Warsaw only as victims is to deny their humanity. Seeing them only as they appear in surviving photos, staring at the camera with infinite sadness, is limiting, both to them and to those who want to understand them. To an object of pity, the only appropriate response becomes "Those poor creatures!" and that reduces both the quality of their struggle and the depth of their despair. No one is served by such two-dimensional views of people and their cultures.

With this in mind, The Way People Live series strives to flesh out the traditional, two-dimensional views of people in various cultures and historical circumstances. Using a wide variety of primary quotations—the words not only of the politicians and government leaders, but of the real people whose lives are being examined—each book in the series attempts to show an honest and complete picture of a culture removed from our own by time or space.

By examining cultures in this way, the reader will notice not only the glaring differences from his or her own culture, but also will be struck by the similarities. For indeed, people share common needs—warmth, good company, stability, and affirmation from others. Ultimately, seeing how people really live, or have lived, can only enrich our understanding of ourselves.

Athens, the "School for Greece"

Over the past few centuries, travelers who have visited Athens and have stood in awe of the still majestic remains of the buildings on its central hill, the Acropolis, have often waxed nostalgic about "the Greek golden age," "the Greek miracle," and "the glory that was Greece." Yet it would perhaps be more accurate to say "the Athenian golden age," "the Athenian miracle," and "the glory that was Athens." For in the fifth and fourth centuries B.C. the period modern historians refer to as Greece's Classic Age, Athens experienced the greatest single burst of political and artistic creativity in human history. "In the course of about 150 years," University of London scholar Sue Blundell remarks,

> the city produced an amazing succession of writers, artists, and thinkers. The dramatists Aeschylus, Sophocles, Euripides and Aristophanes, the historians Herodotus and Thucydides, the sculptors Phidias and Praxiteles, the philosophers Socrates, Plato, and Aristotle—these are just some of the men who lived and worked there during this time. In addition, there were many painters, sculptors and architects employed in the city whose names are frequently unknown to us. In particular, the building program on the Athenian Acropolis, carried out in the second half of the fifth century [B.C.], brought together numerous artists of outstanding caliber.[1]

To the names of these talented individuals can be added those of the many brilliant Athenian political and military leaders of the period, among them Themistocles, Cimon, and Pericles. So instrumental was Pericles in raising Athens to greatness that the mid–fifth century B.C. is often called the "Periclean age" in his honor. Pericles correctly predicted that "future ages will wonder at us, as the present age wonders at us now."[2]

What Pericles did not foresee, however, was how the vast majority of people in those future ages would interpret "us." He and his colleagues considered themselves first and foremost Athenians. And they would undoubtedly be surprised and disconcerted to learn that later generations came so casually to lump them together with other Greeks. After all, in ancient times Greece was never a single nation in the modern sense; rather, it was made up of hundreds of small city-states (and at times kingdoms), each of which considered itself a separate nation and had its own local political and social customs and institutions. Athens, like each of its neighbors, was fiercely proud of its independence and uniqueness, and it frequently fought one or more of its neighbors to maintain its integrity and/or dominance.

Athenian culture became synonymous with Greek culture in the popular consciousness of later ages largely for the same reason that Athens stood out during the Classic Age. For almost two centuries it was the largest, most populous, wealthiest, one of the most powerful, and always the most influential of the Greek city-states. It was also the most openly and staunchly democratic (having instituted the world's first democracy in the late sixth century B.C.). These factors, along with others of a political, economic, and cultural nature, somehow combined in just the right way at the right time to produce something rare, unique, and brilliant. As the late distinguished classical historian C. M. Bowra explains,

> No other Greek state in the middle years of the fifth century can be compared with [Athens] for the range, strength, and originality of her achievement, and indeed she presents the culmination of the many forces which had made the Greeks unique among peoples and given a special character to their outlook and their habits. . . . She embodied all that was most worth having in the civilization of Greece.[3]

Another reason why Athenian culture figures so prominently in modern popular perceptions, as well as serious studies, of ancient Greece is because of the nature of the evidence. Most of the substantial firsthand information that has survived about Greek civilization comes from Athenian writers and other Athenian sources and describes Athenian history, customs, ideas, and so forth. Many other city-states had rich cultures of their own, similar in many ways to that of Athens; however, since evidence for these city-states is mainly scattered and fragmentary, historians have only just begun to piece together reliable pictures of their histories, beliefs, and lifestyles.[4]

It must also be emphasized that a large proportion of the surviving evidence comes from the Classic Age. Ever since the mid–second millennium B.C. (and perhaps earlier),

A restoration of the Athenian Acropolis as it likely appeared at the height of its glory in the late fifth century B.C.

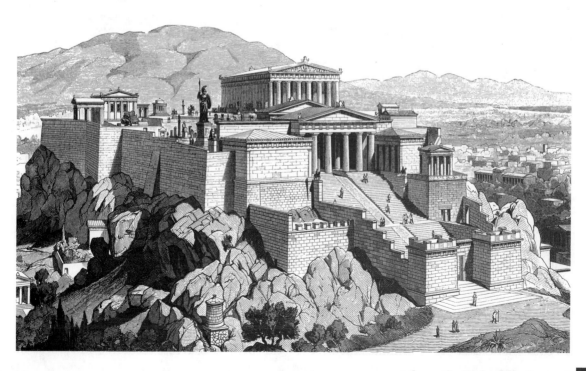

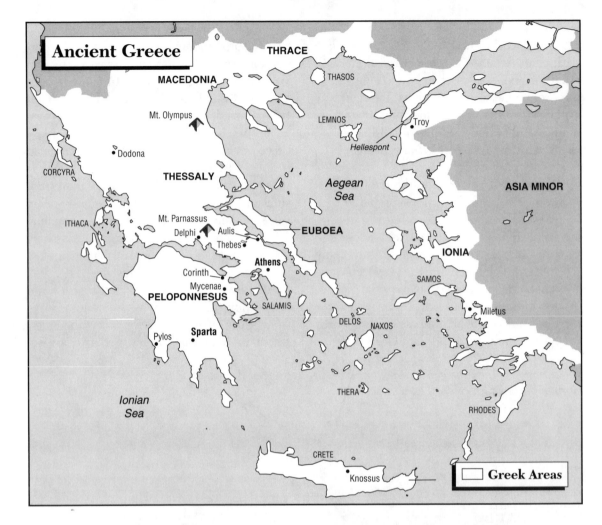

Ancient Greece

THRACE

MACEDONIA

THASOS

Mt. Olympus

LEMNOS

Troy

Dodona

Hellespont

CORCYRA

THESSALY

Aegean Sea

ASIA MINOR

ITHACA

Mt. Parnassus

Delphi Aulis

EUBOEA

Thebes

IONIA

Athens

Corinth

SAMOS

Mycenae

PELOPONNESUS

SALAMIS

Miletus

DELOS NAXOS

Sparta

Pylos

Ionian Sea

THERA

RHODES

Greek Areas

CRETE

Knossos

Athens has been continuously inhabited by Greek-speaking people. Thus, the term *ancient Athens* can refer to the city at any time from about 1600 B.C. (in the Bronze Age, the period in which people used weapons and tools made of bronze) to the fifth and sixth centuries A.D. (when classical, or Greco-Roman, civilization declined, bringing antiquity to a close). During this long period of more than two thousand years, Athenian society and culture steadily evolved and changed. We know about some of these changes, but most remain inadequately documented and therefore uncertain. Because the Classic Age constitutes the best-documented period, this volume deals with Athenian politics, social roles, religious beliefs, artistic endeavors, leisure activities, and military customs during that period; and the reader should not assume that all of the customs, institutions, and ideas described prevailed in Athens throughout antiquity.

Sources of Evidence

The evidence documenting life in classical Athens takes various forms. First, there are the written sources, including the works of historians, principally Herodotus (fifth century B.C.), who wrote about the Greek and Persian wars in which Athens played a major role and the Greek social customs and religious beliefs of his day; Thucydides (fifth century B.C.), who chronicled the disastrous Peloponnesian War that brought Athens to the brink of ruin; and Xenophon (pronounced ZEN-uh-phon; fifth–fourth century B.C.), who continued Thucydides' history of Athens into the fourth century and also discussed social customs, including the duties of women and slaves. "Husbands differ widely in their treatment of their wives," Xenophon writes in *Oeconomicus (The Householder)*, "and some succeed in winning their cooperation . . . while others bring utter ruin on their houses by their behavior toward them."[5]

The renowned, graceful Porch of the Maidens, projecting from the south side of the Erechtheum temple.

Other written sources include the surviving works of Aeschylus and the other great fifth-century B.C. Athenian playwrights. Though their plots are generally fictional and their characters are larger-than-life or satiric, these works often capture or reflect contemporary social mores and religious beliefs. The treatises of philosopher-scientists, most notably Plato, Aristotle, and Theophrastus (all fourth century B.C.), cover a wide range of subjects, ranging from politics and government to religion and morality. Especially valuable are several surviving speeches from the Athenian law courts. Composed by professional writers and orators for average citizens pleading their cases, these speeches not only reveal much legal information but also numerous facts about everyday life. Last, but often not least, are the commentaries of later ancient writers, such as Plutarch (Greek, first–second century A.D.); and Pausanias (Greek, second century A.D.), who had access to sources now lost and/or described sites and buildings that no longer exist.

As any classical scholar will attest, these surviving written sources do not cover all aspects of daily life and are often vague or misleading; this forces scholars to try to fill in the gaps by examining inscriptions, artifacts, and other archaeological evidence. One kind of inscription, the tomb epitaph, is particularly important because it is often the principal source of knowledge about the lives and feelings of those who had no political power or voice— women, children, and slaves. "Chaerestrate lies in this tomb," reads an epitaph found at Piraeus, Athens's port town. "When she was alive, her husband loved her. When she died, he lamented."[6] This is one of the few existing pieces of evidence that at least some Athenian husbands and wives, whose marriages were almost always arranged, actually loved each other.

Other archaeological evidence consists of artifacts such as tools, utensils, jewelry, weapons, coins, and the remains of buildings and animal and human skeletons; bronze or stone sculptures, like those that adorned the Parthenon and other temples, which typically picture gods and humans interacting, sacred processions, and other religious themes;[7] and paintings on vases, cups, and walls, which depict sports and games, music and dance, sexual activities, eating and drinking, clothing styles, armor and warfare, and much more.

Combining all of these kinds of evidence, scholars have pieced together a still incomplete but nevertheless vivid and fascinating picture of life in what was then and still is perceived as the model ancient society. As Pericles told his countrymen, "I say that as a city we are the school [i.e., teacher and premiere example] of Greece; while I doubt if the world can produce a man . . . equal to so many emergencies, and graced by so happy a versatility as

The inner left corner of the Propylaea, the monumental entrance gate of the Athenian Acropolis.

This third-century B.C. *terra-cotta figurine depicts a Greek woman cooking or baking.*

the Athenian."[8] One might easily dismiss this statement as the typical proud boast of a local politician; that is, until one actually visits Athens and climbs the stone steps that rise along the west side of the Acropolis. Upon seeing firsthand what words and pictures can only partly convey—the silent, timeless nobility and grandeur of the Parthenon and other temples on the summit—the traveler inevitably experiences a rush of exhilaration; and from that day forward, he or she realizes how little Pericles exaggerated when he declared:

You must yourself realize the power of Athens, and feast your eyes on her from day to day, till love of her fills your hearts; and then when all her greatness shall break upon you, you must reflect that it was by courage, sense of duty, and a keen feeling of honor in action that men were enabled to win all this.[9]

The Growth of the City-State and Its Government

I n the Classic Age, Athens was one of many city-states that had developed in Greece over the preceding few hundred years. A typical city-state, what the Greeks called a polis (or, when plural, poleis), consisted of a central urban center (town) surrounded by small supporting villages and tracts of farmland. Most of the urban centers were constructed around a hill or cliff known as an acropolis, which in Greek means "the city's high place." Although such towns were physically similar, they evolved different traditions and governments and thought of themselves as separate nations. "Each little plain," noted scholar Alfred Zimmern explains,

> rigidly sealed within its mountain-barriers and with its population concentrated upon its small portion of good soil, seems formed to be a complete world of its own. Make your way up the pastureland, over the pass and down onto the fields and orchards on the other side, and you will find new traditions and customs, new laws and new gods, and most probably a new dialect. You will be in a new nation. . . . You will find a fierce and obstinate national spirit that knows of no allegiance to a sovereign beyond its horizon and regards home rule as the very breath of its being.[10]

In terms of its basic physical setup and independent national spirit, Athens was no different than other Greek poleis. However, a number of factors combined to give classical Athenian culture its unique and special identity and to make Athens the leading state of Greece, then and for all times. Chief among these factors were the city's strategic location, the terrain and climate of its surrounding countryside, a history that over time thrust it into the center of Greek affairs, its freedom-loving citizenry, and the democratic government and legal institutions these people created in the sixth through fourth centuries B.C.

The Attic Peninsula

In ancient times the Athenian polis incorporated all of Attica, a roughly triangular-shaped peninsula jutting from the southeastern sector of the Greek mainland into the blue waters of the Aegean Sea. According to Athenian tradition, the hero Theseus had united the scattered villages of Attica into a single state many centuries before in the fabled "age of heroes" (what modern scholars call the Bronze Age, ending in about 1100 B.C.). Because Attica covers an area of about 965 square miles (2,500 square kilometers), slightly larger than the state of Rhode Island, Athens was unusually large for a Greek state. Over time Athens's size proved highly advantageous. It not only allowed for the growth of a large, diversified population but also provided plentiful quantities of certain important natural resources, notably clay and marble. The clay made possible the production of Athens's highly valued pottery, distributed throughout the eastern Mediterranean sphere, and the marble allowed for the construction of the city's magnificent stone temples.

These advantages aside, at first glance Attica might seem an unlikely place to build a splendid, influential culture. The peninsula is located in the driest part of Greece; its summers are hot and almost rainless, its terrain is rocky and rugged, and its soil is thin. According to Plato,

> There has never been any considerable accumulation of the soil coming down from the mountains, as in other places. . . . The consequence is . . . there are remaining only the bones of the wasted body . . . all the richer and softer parts of the soil having fallen away, and the mere skeleton of the land being left.[11]

By the dawn of the Classic Age, the generally poor Attic soil produced only about half of the grain consumed by Athens's burgeoning population; the rest had to be imported from foreign states, mostly located on the more fertile shores of the Black Sea.

Although hot, arid, and rocky, in Plato's day Attica was dotted by cool springs and shady groves of elms and cypresses. Some crops, chief among them olives, figs, and grapes, even thrived in the local climate and soil. Moreover, the Athenian polis was situated in a geographically strategic position, allowing it easy access to a majority of the important mainland and Aegean poleis, many of which it dominated by the mid–fifth century B.C. Athens's urban center was located about four miles inland from Attica's western coast, along the Saronic Gulf, an inlet of the Aegean. From the port of Piraeus, constructed in the early fifth century on the gulf about five miles southwest of the town, Athenian merchant vessels and warships ventured far and wide, trading a variety of goods and enforcing the will of the Athenian people.

Urban Expansion

Within the valley in which Athens's urban center grew, the most strategic spot was always the Acropolis. Rising nearly four hun-

The huge Corinthian pillars in the foreground are the remains of Athens's Temple of Olympian Zeus, completed in Roman times. The Acropolis, dominated by the Parthenon, rises in the distance.

A Land of Plenty

In contrast to Attica's dry climate and thin soil, many of the Greek city-states bordering the Black Sea (which the Greeks called the Euxine) enjoyed moist climates and rich soils that produced abundant grain. And some of these cities supplied classical Athens with the bulk of its grain. In this excerpt from his *Anabasis,* Xenophon describes the fertile region of Calpe, on the Black Sea's southern shore, not yet a city but filled with potential.

"It is a promontory jutting out into the sea; the part by the sea being a sheer cliff . . . and facing the land a neck about four hundred feet wide. The space inside the neck is enough for ten thousand inhabitants. The harbor under the cliff has a beach towards the west. There is a spring of plentiful sweet water close beside the sea commanded by the promontory. There is [an] abundance of all sorts of wood, and particularly a great deal of fine wood for ship-building close to the sea. The highland stretches into the country some two or three miles, good soil without stones; and the part along the seashore is . . . set thick with timber of all sorts. The rest of the country for a long way round is good. . . . The land bears barley and wheat . . . of all sorts, millet and sesame, figs enough, plenty of grapes, good wine-grapes too, and everything else except olives."

dred feet from the surrounding plain, this huge, rugged limestone rock constituted a natural fortress and formed the nucleus of local settlement as far back as the early Bronze Age. Two other smaller rocky outcrops, the Areopagus ("hill of Ares") and the Pnyx Hill, rose just west of the Acropolis; likewise, a brook, the Eridanos, flowed about half a mile to the north.

Exactly how the city looked in its earliest days is uncertain. Archaeologists have ascertained, however, that by the late Bronze Age, at about the time of the Trojan War (ca. 1200 B.C.), when Greece was made up of small kingdoms (a civilization historians refer to as Mycenaean), the palace of the local king rested atop the Acropolis. At the time most or all of the town's inhabitants apparently lived in caves and small houses at the base of the rock, ready to retreat to the safety of its heights in times of danger.

When Mycenaean civilization collapsed in about 1100 B.C., Athens, like other Greek cities, entered a dark age about which little is known.[12] What is certain is that the town slowly expanded outward from the Acropolis during the centuries that followed. The clefts at the base of the hill came to house shrines for religious cults, old goat paths and footpaths became streets, and people erected houses and other buildings in what had once been outlying family fields. Meanwhile, the flat open area between the Areopagus and Eridanos developed into the Agora, or marketplace; not far beyond it rose a fortified wall that enclosed the whole town (which, in the early sixth century, probably covered a roughly circular area a bit less than a mile across). The Acropolis, upon which the Athenians had built a series of temples and shrines, remained the focal point of religious activities; however, the Agora became the community's heart—the scene of most commercial, legal, and administrative activities.

Athens's urban area underwent some dramatic face-lifts in the Classic Age. In the early

atop the Acropolis. In 478, shortly after the Persians were driven from Greece, the defensive wall was rebuilt, this time with thirteen gates and enclosing an area over a mile-and-a-half wide. Two decades later the Athenians constructed a massive extension, the Long Walls, which stretched the entire five miles to Piraeus, giving the urban center safe access to the sea and the vital grain route. The fifth century also witnessed the construction of new public buildings in the Agora and a magnificent new complex of temples on the Acropolis, crowned by the immortal Parthenon.

The remains of the Athenian Agora and well-preserved Temple of Hephaestos, as seen from the summit of the Acropolis.

Political Experimentation

fifth century an invading force of Persians occupied and destroyed much of the city, including the defensive wall and the temples

In the centuries leading up to the Classic Age, as Athens grew more prosperous and underwent steady physical expansion, it also be-

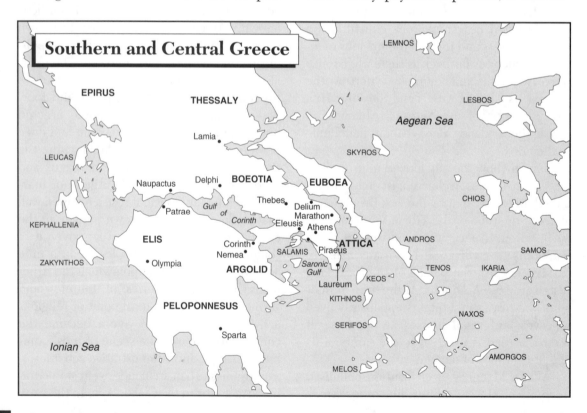

Southern and Central Greece

EPIRUS

THESSALY

LEMNOS

LESBOS

Aegean Sea

Lamia

SKYROS

LEUCAS

Naupactus

Delphi

BOEOTIA

EUBOEA

CHIOS

Thebes

Delium

Marathon

Patrae

Gulf of Corinth

Eleusis

Athens

KEPHALLENIA

ELIS

Corinth

Nemea

SALAMIS

Piraeus

ATTICA

ANDROS

SAMOS

ZAKYNTHOS

Olympia

ARGOLID

Saronic Gulf

KEOS

TENOS

IKARIA

Laureum

KITHNOS

PELOPONNESUS

NAXOS

Sparta

SERIFOS

Ionian Sea

MELOS

AMORGOS

This modern drawing depicts a meeting of the Areopagus, Athens's ancient aristocratic council, whose members were mainly ex-archons who served for life. The council's powers were considerably diluted in the mid–fifth century B.C.

came the scene of increasing political unrest and experimentation. At some unknown date its early kings were replaced by a group of three public administrators, all aristocrats, bearing the title of archon. At first one or more of these served for life, but sometime in the early seventh century B.C. annual elections began. By the middle of that century, six more archons had been added for a total of nine. It remains somewhat unclear who chose them, but most scholars believe they were elected by the Assembly (Ecclesia), a body made up of Athenian landholders who met mainly for this purpose. The Assembly probably had few, if any, other powers at this time.

When the aristocratic archons left office, they were admitted to, and thereafter served for life in, a highly prestigious council named for the hill on which its members met—the Areopagus. The amount of power the Areopagus wielded in this period is uncertain. There is no doubt, however, that the common

people increasingly came to resent the stranglehold the nobles held on government and public affairs. The nobles took a tentative step toward reform by appointing an Athenian named Draco (or Dracon) to create a written law code. Draco's laws were considered too harsh, though, and by the early 500s B.C. Athens tottered on the brink of a bloody social revolution.

In 594, in a last ditch effort to avoid civil war, the opposing groups asked Solon, a citizen with a reputation for wisdom and fairness, to intercede. His solution was a radical legal and social reorganization that gave the common people a true voice in government and thereby paved the way for the emergence of full-blown democracy several decades later. Solon eliminated Draco's repressive laws (except for those dealing with murder); introduced a new social ranking based on wealth rather than birth, making it possible for commoners to rise to the rank of archon; and

A fanciful depiction of Solon, the great sixth-century B.C. Athenian arbitrator, made long after his death. No one knows his true appearance, but it is almost certain he had a beard.

created the Council (Boule), a group of four hundred men, chosen by lot from all classes, who prepared the agenda for the Assembly and served to balance the power of the aristocratic Areopagus. According to Plutarch, Solon himself appraised the historic compromise this way:

> To the mass of the people I gave the power they needed,
>
> Neither degrading them, nor giving them too much rein.
>
> For those who already possessed great power and wealth
>
> I saw to it that their interests were not harmed.
>
> I stood guard with a broad shield before both parties
>
> And prevented either from triumphing unjustly.[13]

Family and Clan

While implementing his reforms, Solon was wise enough not to tamper with the fundamental traditions everyone accepted without question, such as religious beliefs and the basic structure of Athenian society. That structure consisted of a series of concentric social units. These had evolved over the course of centuries and would, with some modifications, remain in effect throughout the Classic Age and beyond.

The smallest and most basic social unit was the family, or *oikos* (plural, *oikoi*). It included not only the members of the "nuclear" family common in modern American society (parents and children) but also grandparents and other relatives, all property, including land and slaves, and the tombs of ancestors. The *oikos* was "the basis of one's security and social identity," explains scholar N. R. E. Fisher, "and the main source of one's social and religious obligations and relationships."[14]

The first such obligation was to make sure that the family did not die out. Since Athenian society was patriarchal (dominated by men), family leadership and property ownership passed from father to son; so it was essential for the head of the family to produce a son or, if necessary, to adopt one. The law "appears to have allowed a man without a son to adopt someone, normally an adult, into his *oikos*," Fisher continues,

> who then left his former *oikos* and resigned any claims to any part of it; the "father" would thus attempt to ensure both the continuation of his line and also that maintenance in old age and performance of correct burial rites which a father who had brought up children could socially and legally demand from them in return.[15]

When the head of the household had more than one son, the sons eventually established their own *oikoi,* which remained linked to the parent family through strong kinship ties. This was the basis of the next largest social group, the clan, or *genos* (plural, *gene*). The average *genos* consisted of a group of families that claimed descent from a common ancestor. In the affairs of the extended family, the heads of the *gene* were usually more influential than the heads of individual households. It was common, for example, for a clan leader to arrange marriages for his various

On reaching manhood, the boy shown in this relief sculpture will likely become the head of his own family unit. But he will still be strongly influenced by his father and clan leader.

This fifth-century B.C. *vase painting shows the generations of an Athenian* oikos, *which was often an extended family that included grandparents as well as parents and children.*

sons, daughters, nephews, nieces, cousins, and grandchildren, who might come from many different *oikoi.*

Phratry, Tribe, and Deme

The next units in the widening social pyramid were the phratry and the tribe, both highly extended kinship groups. The typical phratry, or "blood brotherhood," consisted of about thirty clans, or about as many people as lived in an Attic village or a neighborhood in Athens's urban center. Indeed, many such villages and neighborhoods were dominated by one or two phratries. Often the focus of social gatherings and religious rituals, a phratry was similar to a modern religious congregation, except that the members of a phratry were related to one another. The exceptions to this rule were people who, because of various circumstances, had no family or clans. Phratries sometimes adopted, or welcomed into their ranks, such unfortunate individuals.

The tribe, or *phyle* (plural, *phylai*), the largest single social unit, commonly consisted of three phratries. Until about 508 B.C., Athens had four traditional tribes.[16] At this juncture, however, an influential leader named Cleisthenes spearheaded new political and social reforms that reshaped the old tribal structure. According to Herodotus, Cleisthenes

> changed the number of Athenian tribes from four to ten, and abolished the old names. . . . He named the new tribes after other [mythical] heroes, all native Athenians [Erechthesis, Aegeis, Pandianis, Leontis, Acamantis, Oineis, Cecropis, Hippothontis, Aeantis, and Antiochis] . . . appointing ten [tribal] presidents— *phylarchs*—instead of the original four.[17]

Cleisthenes' reforms also divided Attica into approximately 140 small geographical units, or community districts, called demes (or *demoi*). These districts became the focus of many of the social and religious activities of the phratries and new tribes. The demes and new tribes were arranged in such a way that each tribe contained people from each of Attica's three general regions—the urban area, the coastal areas, and the inland areas.

One reason for this new arrangement was to ensure a more reliable military force. Before, each tribe had provided an unspecified number of soldiers for the army (which was a part-time militia rather than a standing army), and on a more or less voluntary basis. Under the new plan, each of the ten tribes was required to supply a minimum number of troops during a military emergency. This meant that the army would be both larger and drawn more evenly and fairly from all quarters of society. At the same time, the reformers hoped to reduce the influence of the traditional phratries and tribes, which had often feuded among themselves and/or placed their own local interests above those of the polis. Under the new system, Fisher explains, "each man found himself grouped with others from all over Attica, and thus it was hoped that local loyalties, which had been strong and disruptive during the sixth century, might be diminished."[18]

Equality Under the Law

The aim of increasing people's loyalty to the community as a whole, and thereby strengthening the polis, underscored the political aspects of the new reforms. Before initiating them, Cleisthenes, a leading aristocrat, had been involved in a power struggle with rival aristocrats. This reflected the fact that, though Solon's democratic reforms had increased the political power of the middle and lower classes, aristocrats still largely controlled the state. Unlike his opponents, Cleisthenes saw the wisdom of offering the commoners more of a say in government in return for their support; thus, as Herodotus memorably writes, Cleisthenes "took the [common] people into his party."[19]

Thus, the creation of the new tribes and demes, as well as the corresponding reduction in the influence of the phratries and traditional tribes, was first and foremost an attempt to reduce the power of the aristocrats who controlled the older groups. The new system, with its thorough mix of people from all social classes, operated, at least in theory, on the principle of equality under the law (*isonomia*). In the words of prolific classical scholar Michael Grant,

> The *isonomia* of Cleisthenes, though it did not all come into force at once, but emerged gradually, was a sophisticated, intricate, and experimental array of new political institutions, adding up to the most democratic form of government that had so far been devised by human ingenuity, and establishing the essential features of Athenian society for 200 years.[20]

The Assembly and the Citizen Body

The most fundamental of these democratic institutions, the Assembly, in which the citizen body, or *demos,* met, was of course not new.[21] With aristocratic political authority now measurably reduced, however, it possessed considerable powers, which it exercised with increasing boldness in the decades that followed. In addition to directly electing some public officials, the Assembly had the sovereign authority to declare war, make peace, create commercial alliances, grant citizenship, found colonies, allocate public funds for construction and other projects, and decide foreign policy.

The sweeping nature of the Assembly's powers is best illustrated by its wartime responsibilities. The assembled citizens determined the basic strategy, how many soldiers or ships would be employed, and which generals would command. Those generals then planned and carried out the specific battlefield strategies and tactics. No other citizen body in human history, including those of the most liberal modern democracies, has ever wielded so much direct authority in state affairs.

Athens's democracy was decidedly *less* liberal than its modern counterparts, though,

In this mid-sixth-century B.C. *terra-cotta jug painting, executed in the black-figure style, workers (possibly metics or slaves) handle bolts of cloth in a fabric shop.*

in its narrow definition of the term *citizen*. Only free males born in Attica were eligible for complete citizenship rights, including the political rights to vote and hold public office (which required a minimum age of eighteen). Their female relatives were also citizens, but they were a special type called the *astai*—"those without political rights." Slaves, who had no rights at all, could not be citizens; neither could *metics* (*metoikoi*), the foreigners (including both non-Greeks and Greeks from other poleis) who lived and worked in Athens. The *metics* were mostly merchants and tradespeople, such as potters, metalsmiths, and jewelers. The fact that they could neither take part in government nor own land seems unfair by modern standards, since these foreigners made important contributions to the community, including providing essential goods and services, paying taxes, and serving in the army when needed.

Full citizenship was thus a special and cherished right; its loss, known as *atimia* (literally "dishonor"), the stiffest penalty delivered by the courts short of exile or death, was highly dreaded. An *atimos*, a man whose citizenship had been revoked, could not speak in the Assembly or the law courts, hold public office, or enter a temple or the marketplace. And the community as a whole strictly enforced these sanctions; for example, any citizen who saw an *atimos* in a prohibited area was allowed to arrest him on the spot.

But though civic rights were generally cherished in Athens, not all citizens exercised them on a regular basis. Assembly attendance serves as an example. According to some modern estimates, there were approximately 40,000 to 45,000 male adult Athenian citizens in the mid-to-late fifth century B.C. (The rest of Attica's population consisted of about 130,000 female and child citizens, 28,000 *metics,* and 115,000 slaves.) Since close to 30,000 of the male adults lived in the countryside, those that bothered to make the often time-consuming trek into the city to attend Assembly meetings likely did so on an occasional basis. Evidence suggests that in the

Jostling for Seats in the Assembly

This excerpt from Aristophanes' comic play *Acharnians*, written in 425 B.C., when Athens had been embroiled in a disastrous war for almost six years, describes the start of an Assembly meeting from the point of view of a poor farmer who prefers the countryside to the bustling town and longs for peace.

"Here's the fixed Assembly day, and morning come, and no one in the Pnyx. They're in the Agora, chattering up and down, scurrying to dodge the cord dripping red. Why, even the Prytanes [councillors] are not here! They'll come late, elbowing each other, jostling for the front bench. . . . But as for making peace, they do not care one jot. O City! City! But I am always first of all to come, and here I take my seat; then, all alone, I pass the time complaining, yawing, stretching . . . [and] gaze fondly countryward, longing for peace, loathing the town, sick for my village home. . . . So here I'm waiting, thoroughly prepared to riot, wrangle, [and] interrupt the speakers whenever they speak of anything but peace. But here they come, our noon-day Prytanes! . . . I told you how 'twould be; everyone jostling for the foremost place."

The picturesque Hill of the Muses, located about half a mile southeast of Pnyx Hill. The latter was the site of the outdoor meetings of the Athenian Assembly.

fifth century attendance averaged between 4,000 and 5,000 (and 6,000 or more in the fourth century).[22] If too few citizens showed up, a group of 300 specially trained slaves chased shirkers through the streets, swatting their clothes with a rope dipped in red paint. Any man caught with a red stain on his tunic had to pay a fine.

The Assembly met in the morning in the open air on the Pnyx Hill. Historian C. E. Robinson summarizes a typical meeting:

> A herald ordained silence. Prayers were offered by a priest and a black pig was sacrificed. . . . "Who wishes to speak?" cried the herald; and whoever was for addressing the meeting mounted a platform

hewn from the rock. Speeches were followed with eager attention, the audience shouting applause or booing and hissing with displeasure.[23]

The Council and Its Duties

Another institution that was reformed during Cleisthenes' democratic revolution was the Council, which worked in concert with the Assembly by preparing the larger body's agenda. Cleisthenes increased the Council's membership from the four hundred established by Solon to five hundred. University of British Columbia scholar Malcolm F. McGregor tells how these legislators were chosen:

> In the spring of each year the Athenians chose by lot from each of the ten tribes fifty men (a prytany) aged at least thirty to serve on the Council for one year. A councilor (*bouleutes*) drew a small daily fee and was eligible for a second term (but no more) only after an interval (length unknown). This rotation of office meant that each male Athenian might expect to sit in the *Boule* at least once in his life.[24]

A sophisticated system of drawing lots ensured that all areas and interests of Attica were represented. Moreover, the use of this random drawing, coupled with the built-in term limits, effectively deterred the creation of partisan cliques and career politicians in the legislature. This made the Council far more impartial than the Roman Senate or U.S. Congress, in which such groups and individuals were, and remain, facts of life.

The Council's main task was to draw up recommendations (*probouleumata*), similar to legislative bills, that dealt with state business and the community in general. The

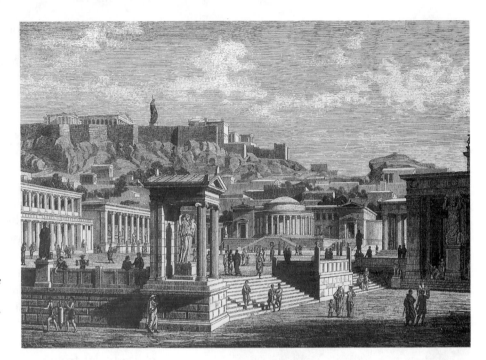

The Council House, or bouleuterion, *was located in the heart of the city, the Agora, pictured in this elegant modern restoration. The temple-studded Acropolis looms impressively in the distance.*

members of the Assembly then debated and voted on these bills. If a majority voted for a bill, it became a decree with the force of law. The Assembly could also change a bill by adding amendments or by sending it back to the Council to be reframed; likewise, the voters could reject the bill outright.

The Council also made sure that the decisions made by the Assembly were duly carried out by overseeing the financial and other administrative business of the community. This task was accomplished by various Council subcommittees (boards of councillors), which closely supervised the magistrates (public officials), beginning with the nine archons.[25] In his description of Athens's government, Aristotle provides this example of such a subcommittee in action:

> The Council also inspects triremes [warships] after construction, and their rigging, and the naval shed, and has new triremes . . . voted for by the Assembly,

built and rigged, and naval sheds built; but naval architects are elected by the Assembly. . . . For the building of the triremes it elects ten of its own members as Naval Constructors. It also inspects all public buildings, and if it finds any commissioner in default, it reports him to the Assembly, and if it gets a verdict of guilty hands him over to a jury-court.[26]

Other Democratic Institutions and Procedures

One new and very important institution introduced by Cleisthenes was the Strategia, a board of ten generals (*strategoi;* or, when singular, *strategos*), directly elected by the Assembly. Like the councillors, archons, and other officials, the *strategoi* served for a year; unlike the others, however, the generals could be reelected immediately and for an unlimited number of terms. This system was based on the wisdom that frequently overhauling the military leadership during a war or other national emergency could prove dangerous or even disastrous.

Under the new democracy, an Athenian general was much more than just a military leader. The *strategoi* became leading speakers in the Assembly, could initiate policy both there and in the Council (which explains why many decrees had the names of generals, such as Cimon or Pericles, attached to them), had the power to convene an Assembly meeting, and carried out the Assembly's foreign policy initiatives. When reelected frequently, a popular general was the most influential and powerful member of the community. (The most conspicuous example was Pericles, who was elected *strategos* over twenty times, fifteen of them consecutively between 443 and 429 B.C.)

The influence of even the most popular general was limited, however, because the system featured highly effective procedures for making public officials accountable and removing them from office. Before serving, each candidate had to undergo a rigorous examination (*dokimasia*) that considered his character as well as his other qualifications. At any time during his term, citizens could charge him with abuse of office and bring him before the Assembly, which could fine him, remove him from office, or even condemn him to death. In addition, a procedure known as ostracism was designed both to prevent one leader from amassing too much power and to allow the citizens to remove a leader whose policies they felt were hindering the decision-making process. Professor McGregor explains how ostracism worked:

> Each year the Athenians voted . . . whether to hold an ostracism. In the event of an affirmative vote, the citizens, a few weeks later but before elections (in the early spring), reassembled. Each one scratched on a shard [a piece of broken pottery called an *ostrakon*] the name of the man who seemed most to threaten [political] stability; such, at any rate, is the theory [because the exact procedure is still uncertain]. He who polled the most votes (6,000 had to be cast) withdrew from the polis for ten years without loss of property or citizenship.[27]

This ostrakon *is one of many found bearing Themistocles' name. Evidently, his political opponents made several unsuccessful attempts to oust him before finally succeeding about 472 B.C.*

Athenian Justice

A large portion of the democracy's machinery was devoted to administering justice. Each year six thousand men at least thirty years of age were chosen by lot to serve as jurors, or dicasts (*dikastai*). They tended to be elderly and, thanks to legislation initiated by Pericles, received a daily fee (two obols, raised to three in the late 400s). The practice of paying jurors ensured that even the poorest Athenians who wanted to serve could do so and also, as the comic playwright Aristophanes suggested, constituted a sort of old age pension for many citizens.

The courts in which these jurors sat operated differently than those in modern democracies. First, there was no judge; rather, the public magistrate in charge simply made sure that the charges were properly registered and kept order. Penalties were usually prescribed by law, but in some cases the prosecution could suggest one penalty and the defense another; the jurors then decided which sentence to impose. This happened, for example, in 399 B.C. at the famous trial of the philosopher Socrates, who had been accused of corrupting the youth of the community. His jury, which numbered about five hundred, voted twice, the first time to decide his guilt or innocence and the second to choose his penalty. The majority prevailed, and its decision was final—there were no appeals.[28] (The use of such a large number of jurors, which was typical of most trials, was designed to make it impractical, if not impossible, for someone to bribe or threaten enough of them to influence the verdict.)

A modern drawing depicts Socrates addressing the jury at his famous trial. He was eventually condemned to death and soon afterward availed himself of the option of drinking poison in his prison cell.

A Victim Pleads for Justice

This excerpt from Kathleen Freeman's *The Murder of Herodes and Other Trials from the Athenian Law Courts* focuses on the conclusion of a speech written by Demosthenes for the prosecution in a trial that took place in about 340 B.C. The plaintiff-prosecutor, a young man named Ariston, calls on the jurors to convict an older man named Conon, who allegedly harassed and bodily assaulted him.

"I do not swear falsely, no, not though Conon bursts himself to prove it! I therefore call upon you, gentlemen, since I have put before you everything I am justified in pleading, and have supported my case with a solemn oath, to do as you would if you experienced what I have. Just as each of you would hate his attacker, so now in my behalf show your anger towards Conon. . . . Whenever such a thing happens to anyone, come to his aid, mete out punishment, and regard with hatred those who . . . care neither for their good name nor for social usage nor anything else whatever, except only to avoid the penalty! Conon will importune [beg] you and shed tears. But consider which of us is the more deserving of pity: the man who suffers injuries like mine . . . or Conon if he pays the penalty? . . . I do not see that I need say any more. All of you, I believe, are fully aware of what I have told you."

Socrates was convicted and received a death sentence. Other common penalties, depending on the severity of the offense, included imprisonment, exile, partial or full loss of citizenship, confiscation of property, and monetary fines. By modern standards, punishment was severe; even receiving a fine was no trivial matter, for until it was paid in full the offender and all of his descendants were barred from voting, holding public office, or sitting on juries.

Another major way in which an Athenian trial differed from a modern one was the absence of lawyers, either public prosecutors or defense attorneys. There were also no detectives or investigators to gather evidence. The litigants had to gather their own evidence and witnesses and plead their own cases before the jurors. Because many of the litigants did not feel competent to prepare their court speeches, upon which winning or losing hinged, it became common to hire professional speechwriters (*logographai*). Among the most skilled of such writers, many of whom became famous orators, were Antiphon (480–411 B.C.), Lysias (ca. 459–ca. 380), Isaeus (ca. 420–350) and Demosthenes (384–322).

The Athenian Spirit

The emergence of people's courts, assemblies, councils, and other democratic institutions in Athens marked a momentous awakening in human political thinking. For the first time in history, the people did not bend to the will of a monarch or privileged group of nobles but instead had the means to chart their own destiny. When, in Aeschylus's play *The Persians*, the Persian queen asks what master the Athenians obey, she is surprised and confused by the answer: "Master? They are not called servants to any man."[29] The Athenian democratic spirit bred a respect for individual freedom and dignity as well as intense feelings of patriotism. It also encouraged individual creative expression, which in part explains why Athens achieved cultural greatness in the Classic Age.

Moreover, most Athenians did not take their system and the freedoms it guaranteed for granted. It was considered an honor to sustain that system by serving the community. "Although the Athenians valued wealth and material goods as we do," noted historian Donald Kagan points out, "they regarded economic life and status as less noble and important than distinction in public service."[30]

Athenians who never became involved in such service were often viewed with disdain. "We regard the citizen who takes no part in these [public] duties not as unambitious, but as useless,"[31] Pericles declared, giving voice to an attitude far less common in modern democracies. As Kagan eloquently phrases it, to understand the Athenians, "we must study them with humility. For in spite of their antiquity, they may have believed things we have either forgotten or never known; and we must keep open the possibility that in some respects, at least, they were wiser than we."[32]

The Household and the Lives of Its Members

Whether in the countryside or the town, the home was the focus of Athenian family life. As might be expected, the male head of an *oikos*, or family, was also head of the household. Though he might take advice from, or answer to, more senior members of his clan or phratry, in his own home his word was law; he decided how the home would run, enforced the rules, distributed money to family members, hired servants or bought slaves, and arranged for his children's education. His wife, children, other live-in relatives, and slaves were expected to carry out their respective duties and to obey him. Thus, the home, with its leader and subordinates, was like a miniature version of the polis (in which the *demos* made the decisions and individual members of the community did their various duties). "A large household may be compared to a small state,"[33] Plato suggested.

This does not mean that every household head was a petty tyrant who spent most of his time at home ordering everyone around. Most Athenian men spent little time in their homes, which they used mainly for sleeping and eating. Outdoor work occupied most of a farmer's day, for instance, and townsmen were most often found in the marketplace, the law courts, the gymnasium, or traveling from one part of Attica to another. "I certainly do not pass my time indoors," says an Athenian gentleman named Ischomachus in Xenophon's *Oeconomicus*, "for, you know, my wife is quite capable of looking after the house by herself."[34]

Ischomachus's remark captures a basic reality of Athenian life, namely that a man's wife (or mother or other female relative if he was not married) actually ran the household on a day-to-day basis. The sad facts are that Athenian women were second-class citizens who had no political rights and who were often confined to their homes. But this does not

Artifacts like this fourth-century B.C. terra-cotta statuette show how Greek women dressed and wore their hair.

mean that their social roles were insignificant or that they felt their lives unfulfilled. A woman's role and responsibilities within the home were as important to the household's success as her husband's and father's were, on a larger scale, to the success of the polis. Xenophon indicates that marriage and the keeping of a home constituted ideally, and perhaps often in reality, more of a partnership than a dictatorship. "It seems to me, dear," Ischomachus tells his wife,

> that the gods with great discernment have coupled together male and female . . . chiefly in order that they may form a perfect partnership in mutual service. For in the first place, that the various species of living creatures may not fail, they are joined in wedlock for the production of children. Secondly, offspring to support them in old age is provided by this union, to human beings at any rate. . . . And since both the indoor and the outdoor tasks demand labor and attention, God from the first adapted the woman's nature, I think, to the indoor and man's to the outdoor tasks and cares. . . . We must endeavor, each of us, to do the duties allotted to us as well as possible.[35]

Construction and Layout of Houses

Modern scholars know relatively little about the physical appearance of the Athenian homes that the men owned and the women managed. This is because surviving written sources provide no detailed descriptions and the meager remains of only a few such structures have been excavated. When attempting to reconstruct ancient houses, says noted classicist Ian Jenkins,

the archaeologist is faced with scanty or uncertain evidence. Usually nothing survives above ground and perhaps only the indication of where a building once stood is a murky outline staining the earth. Scattered debris may indicate how the walls were constructed and the roof covered. Anything that could be salvaged from the house, however, is likely to have been removed in antiquity. Stone foundations, for example, are liable to have been robbed and used elsewhere.[36]

What seems certain is that the vast majority of Athenian houses, including those of well-to-do families, were simple in design and smaller and more modestly furnished than the average modern family dwelling. Likewise, they were tiny and pitifully unadorned in comparison to public buildings like the Stoa Poikile ("Painted Stoa"), a long colonnaded building decorated with large paintings that stood in the Agora, or magnificent temples like the Acropolis's Parthenon and Erechtheum. If no traces of these larger, finer structures had survived, modern researchers might have concluded that Athens was a primitive, backward place. Indeed, Jenkins remarks, the appearance of classical Athenian houses "belied the great age in which their inhabitants lived."[37]

Like houses throughout Greece, Attic dwellings typically featured a stone foundation and walls made of sun-dried clay bricks. Although the bricks were sometimes reinforced with wooden timbers, the walls were neither strong nor durable. The mud bricks began to crumble after a few years, forcing home owners to undertake frequent repairs. In poorer homes, especially in the countryside, the floors might consist of earth beaten hard and covered with straw mats, layers of pebbles, or perhaps flagstones. Wealthier

Athenians used mosaic tiles and rugs imported from Asia Minor (what is now Turkey). Roofs were most often made of baked pottery tiles.

The general layout of houses in Attica depended to some degree on whether they were country or town houses. Both varieties featured a central courtyard, roofless to take advantage of natural lighting. Some such courtyards had wells to provide a ready water supply, and most, if not all, had small altars at which the family members prayed. Most of the nicer country homes, what we would call villas, featured larger courtyards as well as roofed walkways and gardens along their outer perimeters. At least some, and possibly most, had defensive towers as well; far from the urban center's protective walls and Acropolis, the family had to have a safe refuge in case of sudden danger.[38]

In the urban center, by contrast, the houses were crammed together along narrow winding streets since space was at a premium. Those doors that opened outward were also narrow, so as not to interrupt traffic, and few if any windows faced the streets. The only decoration in the front exterior was perhaps a herm, a bust of the god Hermes resting on a pedestal about three or four feet high, near the door. Among other things, Hermes was the patron of travelers, and it was thought that his likeness kept evil from entering the house.

Inside the Household

House interiors were also simple in design. The poorest homes probably had no courtyard and featured one large room, containing

This restoration of a country house in Attica includes a herm out front. Even the villas and townhouses of the rich were relatively small and unadorned by today's standards.

the hearth, flanked by one or two smaller rooms. Middle- and upper-class homes consisted of a group of small rectangular rooms arranged around, and facing into, the rectangular courtyard. These rooms included the exedra, a sitting area with one side open to the inner court to take advantage of fresh air and natural light; the kitchen, which had an open hearth for cooking, tables for food preparation, and storage bins; and bedrooms, probably one for the master and his wife, one for the children (although the eldest son might have his own room), and one for the household slaves.

The lighting and heating of these rooms was primitive by today's standards. Oil lamps (small shallow vessels that burned wicks fueled by olive oil) and candles (often set in a multiple-candle holder called a candelabra) were the chief lighting devices. Heat was provided by the household hearths and also by braziers, metal containers that burned charcoal. The latter were small and portable, making them easy to move from room to room. For the most part, though, on the coolest nights the warmest place in an Athenian house was beneath one's blankets.

The average home also had a bathroom, which commonly contained a tub, slightly smaller than modern versions, made of terracotta (baked clay). Usually, the family slaves used buckets to fill the tub, which drained to the outside through a channel recessed in the floor; however, a few well-to-do homes may have featured showers, with water carried in by clay pipes. As depicted in a painting on a fourth-century B.C. vase, such modern-looking showers existed in at least some local gymnasiums. Many Athenian bathrooms had terra-cotta toilets as well; in the fifth century these emptied into stone-lined cesspools, but by the fourth century many were connected to an increasingly complex public sewer system. In those homes without a toilet, it was necessary to use a chamber pot, which had to be emptied by hand into the sewer.

Upper middle-class and well-to-do Athenian houses had, in addition, a special room called an *andron*. Here, the head of the household held banquets and entertained his male guests in after-dinner parties called symposia. The men reclined on couches during the preliminary meal, which was served by slaves. Afterward, the host and his guests drank wine, conversed, told stories and riddles, sang songs, or played games. One of the most popular parlor games was *cottabos,* in which the players tried to flip the wine dregs from the bottoms of their cups at a guest's cup, a bowl or vase resting on a pedestal, or some other target; or they attempted, via their tosses, to fill and sink a small dish floating in a large bowl. In addition, it was common for the host to bring in outside entertainers, including *hetairai,* high-class, highly educated prostitutes. Xenophon mentions other entertainers in a work appropriately titled *The Symposium:*

> When the dining tables were removed . . . a certain man from Syracuse [a Greek polis located on the Italian island of Sicily] came in to furnish entertainment, having as his assistants [in this case all slaves] a girl skilled in playing the flute, a dancing girl marvelously adept at acrobatics, and a boy at the peak of his beauty, skilled in playing the lyre [a small harp] and in dancing. By exhibiting them in their marvelous performance, the owner earned a living.[39]

Women's Duties and Expected Behavior

It is important to note that the host's wife, daughters, mother, or sisters did not take part in symposia or other such gatherings; for it was considered unseemly for them to be seen by, let alone to mix with, visiting males who were not a part of their *oikos.* At such times, and also when appropriate during the normal course of each day, the ladies of the house retired to the *gynaeceum* (or *gynaikonitis*), meaning the "women's quarters." Depending on the size of the house, this consisted of one or more large utility rooms (located in the

This modern depiction of Athenian women's quarters considerably exaggerates their size, splendor, and frivolous use. Most were small, spare, work-oriented facilities.

back of single-story houses and upstairs in those with two stories) in which they engaged in spinning, weaving, and visiting with female guests. The Roman writer Cornelius Nepos, who visited Athens not long after the Classic Age, found such segregation of women odd and compared it unfavorably to the custom in his own society:

> Many actions are seemly according to our [i.e., the Roman] code which the Greeks look upon as shameful. For instance, what Roman would blush to take his wife to a dinner-party? What matron does not frequent the front rooms of her dwelling and show herself in public? But it is very different in [Athens]; for there a woman

The Household and the Lives of Its Members

This more realistic restoration of the women's quarters of an average Athenian home shows the women of the house engaging in routine household duties while a slave loads a laundry basket.

is not admitted to a dinner-party, unless relatives only are present, and she keeps to the more retired part of the house called "the women's apartment," to which no man has access who is not near of kin.[40]

Yet though they kept to their quarters while the master was entertaining guests, the women almost certainly had the run of the house the rest of the time. After all, a wife had important duties that she could not have performed if she were locked away all day in the *gynaeceum*. As Xenophon's character Ischomachus points out, these were traditionally indoor duties, including, in addition to spinning and weaving, helping to prepare meals, overseeing the children and servants, paying the bills, and in general keeping the home clean and well-organized. "Your duty will be to remain indoors," Ischomachus tells his wife,

> and send out those servants whose work is outside, and superintend those who are to work indoors, and to receive the incomings [household moneys] and distribute

[pay] as much of them as must be spent. . . . And when wool is brought to you, you must see that the cloaks are made for those [family members] that need them. . . . You will [also] have to see that any servant who is ill is cared for.[41]

In keeping with their indoor role, the women in middle- and upper-class households did not normally work outside, shop, or run errands. But as Professor Sue Blundell points out, poorer women did:

> For many women of the lower classes, complete confinement to the home would not have been feasible. . . . In those homes where there was no well in the courtyard, and no slave to fetch water, women would have to go to the public fountain. The female chorus in Aristophanes' *Lysistrata* (327–331) speaks of the crowd that gathers round the fountain in the morning, and scenes like this are also depicted in vase paintings; there is no reason to assume that all the women represented in these are . . . slaves, aliens,

Here, from their controversial book *Who Killed Homer?*, noted classical scholars Victor D. Hanson and John Heath suggest that a major reason for the development and perpetuation of Athenian women's traditional and strictly observed household roles was that life was hard and the family's and society's survival were uncertain.

"Women had to bear children constantly because most of their offspring did not reach puberty. Sex roles in the household were brutally delineated [sharply defined] because failure to deepen a well or the inability to produce a warm cloak spelled catastrophe. Rote and custom and role-playing reign—as Xenophon reminds us in his *Oeconomicus*—while experimentation and divergence were to be avoided. For a culture always only one harvest short of Armageddon, one child's death away from familial extinction, time-honored sexual roles that provide survival are sacrosanct [sacred] and better left unchanged until the storehouse is full and the population healthy. Most Athenian women were pregnant or nursing [during most of their childbearing years], hoping that about half of those pregnancies would come to term, that half again might just result in healthy infants, that half again of those would survive past the age of three. Unlike us, the Athenians knew that before a utopia . . . of gender equality could be realized, the citizenry first had to figure out how to eat regularly, maintain safety, and stay free of foreign attack."

The cycle of life for Athenian women is illustrated in this exquisite relief showing a baby, mother, and grandmother.

or courtesans [prostitutes]. Lower-class women also went out to work, and even where they were employed indoors (for example, as midwives), they would of course have had to leave the house in order to get to their jobs.[42]

Furthermore, all free Athenian women, regardless of social class, were allowed to attend funerals, public religious festivals (in which they played important roles), and probably the theater. On such occasions, most were likely accompanied by a male family member and took care to avoid conversing with unrelated men, as polite custom dictated.

Love, Marriage, and Divorce

Such segregation and strict supervision of a large proportion of women in society raises the question of how women were able to meet eligible men, fall in love, and decide to get married. The answer is that this familiar courting process is a relatively modern one. As a rule, Athenian marriages were arranged, either by fathers or clan leaders, and it was not unusual for a young bride and groom barely to know each other before their wedding night. Marriage was not a woman's decision, therefore, and social customs surrounding marriage did not encourage or even take into consideration the notion of falling in love. Some evidence suggests that romantic love did exist, but probably few couples were fortunate enough to experience it.

On the whole, marriage was most often a legal arrangement made by men—the prospective bride's father or other male guardian (*kyrios*) and the prospective husband (who became her *kyrios* when he married her). The deal was made at the formal betrothal (*engue*), usually in front of witnesses. Along with the woman, valuable assets changed hands in the form of her dowry (money her father provided for her maintenance). "The Athenians were protective of their women," writes respected scholar Sarah Pomeroy.

A woman's dowry was to remain intact throughout her lifetime and to be used for her support; neither her father, nor her guardian, nor her husband, nor the woman herself could legally dispose of it. Upon marriage, the dowry passed from the guardianship of the father to that of the groom. The groom could use the principal [original sum] but was required to maintain his wife from the income of her dowry, computed at 18 percent annually. Upon divorce, the husband was required to return the dowry to his ex-wife's guardian, or pay interest at 18 percent. Thus her support would often continue to be provided for, and, with her dowry intact, she would be eligible for remarriage.[43]

The need to provide young women with dowries had many social implications. For example, a father was unlikely to raise more daughters than he could afford to supply dowries for, so he might on occasion leave a female infant outside to die of exposure; a wealthy man might supply a poorer man in his clan or phratry with the money needed to establish a dowry; and a man who was heavily in debt might view marriage to a woman with a substantial dowry as a solution to his money troubles.

After the marriage arrangement was sealed, plans for the wedding celebration (*gamos*) began. Shortly before the wedding, the bride collected her childhood toys and the girdle that she had worn since puberty and offered them as a sacrifice to Artemis, the virgin goddess thought to protect young girls and pregnant women. No complete descriptions of the ceremony itself have survived; however, Professor Blundell provides this credible scenario, pieced together from various literary and visual sources:

The public part of the ceremony began with a wedding feast in the house of the bride's father. At nightfall, the partially veiled bride, the groom and the groom's best friend [*parochos*] were carried to the couple's future home in a nuptial chariot

In this drawing, based on a vase painting, an Athenian bride is dressed and groomed for her wedding ceremony. Per custom, she first took a special prenuptial bath.

drawn by mules, accompanied by a torch-lit procession of friends and relatives singing nuptial hymns. . . . At their destination the bride was greeted by her mother-in-law, who was carrying torches, and was formally conducted to the hearth, the focal point of her new home. Meanwhile, bride and groom were showered with nuts and dried fruits, emblems of fertility and prosperity, and a boy crowned with a wreath of thorns and acorns circulated among the guests distributing bread from a basket. . . . The climax of the proceedings came when the bride was led by the groom towards the bridal chamber, while a wedding hymn was sung by the guests. . . . On the following day . . . gifts were presented to the couple by the bride's father and other relatives.[44]

If an Athenian marriage did not work out, divorce was an easily obtainable option with no social stigma attached. When a man initiated the divorce, he simply sent his wife from the house, usually to live with her male relatives (customarily he retained custody of the children). A woman who wanted a divorce had to acquire the aid of a male relative (or some other male citizen) who, on her behalf, brought the case before an archon.

As is true in modern society, one common reason for divorce was adultery (*moicheia*). This was seen as a much more serious offense in ancient Athens than it is today, however, mainly because it cast doubt on the legitimacy of the children and brought shame to the whole family. A woman who committed adultery lived the rest of her life in a state of disgrace and could lose her cherished right to

The Household and the Lives of Its Members **37**

This ornate carved relief of a married couple, which adorned their grave marker, dates from ca. 340–330 B.C.

eral, childhood was not viewed as an enviable, happy time of life, as it often is today, and adults felt little or no nostalgia for their youth. This was partly because they believed that children lacked proper reasoning powers, courage, or even a moral capacity until they were at least in their teens. And so, it was thought, young children needed to be closely watched, carefully trained, and, when necessary, harshly disciplined by parents, tutors, and other community members. After casually grouping children together with animals and slaves, Plato writes,

> Of all animals the boy is the most unmanageable, insomuch as his fountain of reason is not yet regulated. He is the most . . . insubordinate of animals. And that is why he must be bound with many bridles; in the first place, when he gets away from mothers and nurses, he must be under the management of tutors on account of his childishness and foolishness. . . . Any freeman who comes in his way may punish him . . . if he does anything wrong; and he who . . . does not inflict upon him the punishment he deserves shall incur the greatest disgrace.[46]

Children were born at home, and all the women of the *oikos*, often along with a midwife to help with the delivery, were present. A child's guardian (usually the father) remained close by to decide whether to keep or expose it.[47] If kept, two postbirth purification ceremonies celebrated the infant's acceptance into the *oikos*. According to Mark Golden, an authority on Athenian children,

> The *amphidromia*, which took place on the fifth or seventh day after birth, involved a sacrifice; the father (naked according to one late source) carried the

take part in religious festivals. Male adulterers could be prosecuted by the wife's male relatives. Likewise, a husband who actually caught another man with his wife was allowed by law to kill the offender on the spot (unless someone could prove that he had some other motive for the killing, in which case the husband could be prosecuted for murder[45]).

Children and Education

The ideal outcome of marriage, of course, was to produce children to perpetuate the *oikos*. Child-rearing customs reflected a general view of children that most people today would deem misguided and counter to the development of healthy self-esteem. In gen-

child around the household hearth. . . . Friends and relations sent traditional gifts, octopuses and cuttlefish [squid], but did not attend unless they had been present at birth. . . . Girls and the children of poorer families might be named at the same rite. However, those who could . . . bear the extra expense bestowed the name at a second celebration, on the tenth day after birth, the *decate.* This, too, involved an offering to the gods, but was rather more festive—it featured a dance by women, who were rewarded with a special cake—and open . . . to outsiders.[48]

As Athenian children grew, they played with toys familiar to modern children, such as balls (*sphairai*), hoops, tops, dolls (made of wood, clay, or rags) and dollhouses (complete with furniture), yo-yos, and miniature carts and chariots (the equivalent of today's toy cars and trucks). Young boys also began attending school at about age seven. (Young girls were trained at home by their mothers in weaving and other household arts, although some vase paintings suggest that at least a few girls learned to read.) The boys attended private schools in which they learned reading and writing from teachers called *grammatistes.* Once a boy could read, he began absorbing the verses of Homer (the legendary author of the epic poems the *Iliad* and the *Odyssey*) and other poets. According to Plato,

> When the boy has learned his letters . . . they put into his hands the works of great poets, which he reads sitting on a bench at school; in these are contained many pieces of advice, and many tales, and praises and glorification of ancient famous men, which he is required to learn by heart, in order that he may imitate . . . and desire to become like them.[49]

This school scene, painted on a vase, shows young boys doing their lessons under the watchful eyes of their instructors. All students learned to recite long tracts of Homer's works.

Boys also learned to sing and play the lyre (*lyra*) from teachers known as *kitharistes,* and physical education (athletic events and dancing) from *paidotribes.* Some fathers had a slave or freedman (freed slave), called a *paidagogos,* escort their sons to school and supervise their behavior there.

Slaves in the Home and in Society

Paidagogos was only one of many roles and jobs filled by slaves in Athenian homes and society in general. In fact, a large proportion of the physical labor in all social areas and occupations was performed by slaves. (Slaves and free men often worked side by side on Attic farms or urban construction projects. This reflected the common view that it was acceptable for free persons to perform such work as long as they were working for themselves; however, if they were working for someone else, they were no better than slaves.) Like other ancient peoples, including all Greeks, the Athenians accepted the institution of slavery as ordained by the gods and part of the natural way of things. Even great thinkers like Plato and Aristotle, who envisioned utopian societies in their writings (Plato's *Republic,* for example), could not imagine a society operating efficiently without slave labor. And the slaves themselves thought no differently, for the few slaves who managed to earn their freedom immediately acquired slaves of their own.

Athenian slaves were typically captured in wars or bought from slave traders. Because Greeks usually frowned on enslaving other

Certain People Are Slaves by Nature

This excerpt from Aristotle's *Politics* offers a definition of a slave and argues that slavery is part of nature's design.

"A human being who by nature does not belong to himself but to another person— such a one is by nature a slave. A human being belongs to another when he is a piece of property as well as being human. A piece of property is a tool which is used to assist some activity, and which has a separate existence of its own. . . . All men who differ from one another by as much as the soul differs from the body or man from a wild beast (and that is the state of those who work by using their bodies . . .)—these people are slaves by nature, and it is better for them to be subject to this kind of control. . . . For a man who is able to belong to another person is by nature a slave (for that is why he belongs to someone else). . . . Nature must therefore have intended to make the bodies of free men and of slaves different also; slaves' bodies strong for the services they have to do, those of free men upright and not much use for that kind of work, but instead useful for community [i.e., political] life. . . . Of course the opposite often happens—slaves can have the bodies of free men, free men only the souls and not the bodies of free men. After all, it is clear that if they were born with bodies as admirable as the statues of the gods, everyone would say that those who were inferior would deserve to be the slaves of these men. . . . To conclude: it is clear that there are certain people who are free and certain who are slaves by nature, and it is both to their advantage, and just, for them to be slaves."

Slaves commonly did much of the manual labor in local industries. This small clay model depicts four such laborers kneading dough in a bakery while a flute player (whose instrument is missing) provides a tune to set their pace.

Greeks, most slaves in Athens were *barbarians,* the prevailing term for non-Greeks. They came mostly from Asia Minor or from Thrace and other regions lying north of the Aegean Sea. A family of moderate means probably kept two or three slaves, a well-to-do household might have fifteen to twenty, and shops and other commercial enterprises kept even more. An Athenian *metic* named Cephalus, for example, used about 120 slaves in his prosperous shield-making business. The state also owned slaves, which it used in its silver mines at Laureum in southern Attica. Mine slaves, who were shackled day and night, worked in horrendous conditions, and had no hope of gaining freedom, represented the darker side of Athenian slavery.

Household slaves, by contrast, were generally well treated and often became trusted members of the family. Although some owners no doubt hit or flogged such slaves, the law usually prevented severe brutality. Therefore, a free person who beat or killed another person's slave could be prosecuted. Household slaves also often received small wages that they could either spend or save up to buy their freedom, which also might be granted by a kind master as a reward for long years of trusted service. Athenian freedmen had the same social status as *metics,* which meant that they had no political rights. Also like *metics,* however, they were free to become as successful as they desired, and a few did. For instance, a freedman named Paison was the richest manufacturer in Athens and left behind a valuable estate when he died in 370 B.C.

Such success stories remained exceptional, however, for the vast majority of Athenian slaves never gained their freedom. The lucky ones were those who, through circumstances they could not control, found more or less comfortable niches in the homes of kind, or at least fair-minded, masters. There, a slave performed his or her expected tasks for the maintenance and perpetuation of the *oikos,* of which the master was the financial backer, the mistress the manager, the children the future, and the slaves the strong arms.

Religious Beliefs, Festivals, and Customs

Religious belief and worship was one of the most essential aspects of Athenian life. The Athenians had their own special religious festivals and holidays, as did their neighbors in other Greek states, and as Christians, Jews, Muslims, and others do today. The largest Athenian festival, the Panathenaea, was so splendid that it drew participants and spectators not only from all parts of Attica but from all over Greece as well.

In addition, religious rituals, particularly prayer and/or sacrifice, accompanied nearly every Athenian gathering, function, or important endeavor, both private and public. No pious Athenian consumed a meal, for example, without offering a portion of the food to the gods; religious ritual attended important life-cycle events such as birth, marriage, and death; a military general performed a sacrifice before a battle; and meetings of the Assembly began with an animal sacrifice and prayers led by the herald. Major speeches delivered in the Assembly, Agora, the courts, or elsewhere, also often opened with prayers. One of the most famous speeches given by the great orator Demosthenes, *On the Crown* (330 B.C.), starts with these words to a jury:

> I begin, men of Athens, by praying to every God and Goddess that the same goodwill, which I have ever cherished toward . . . all of you, may be requited [repaid] to me on the present trial. I . . . call the Gods to my aid; and in your presence I implore them . . . that they may direct you to such a decision upon this indictment, as will conduce [contribute] to your common honor, and to the good conscience of each individual.[50]

Moreover, the Athenians drew a connection between religion and patriotism in their belief that the gods showed goodwill toward Athens or favored it above other cities. In a similar way, many modern Americans believe that God favors and blesses the United States and preserves and protects it against its ene-

The Athenian Calendar

Each Greek city-state had a different calendar with its own local names of the months, which were often named after religious festivals. These are the Athenian (Attic) months, along with approximate modern equivalents:

Hekatombaion (July)
Metageitnion (August)
Boedromion (September)
Pyanopsion (October)
Maimakterion (November)
Poseideon (December)
Gamelion (January)
Anthesterion (February)
Elaphebolion (March)
Mounichion (April)
Thargelion (May)
Skirophorion (June)

Zeus, leader of the Greek gods, is depicted in this bronze statue dated to ca. 450 B.C. His right hand once held a thunderbolt, one of his chief symbols.

mies. Xenophon puts just such an idea into words in his *Hellenica,* in which an Athenian patriot describes fighting to preserve the democracy against its enemies:

> The gods are quite evidently on our side now. In the middle of fair weather they send us a snowstorm to help us, and when we attack, few against many, it is we who are granted the right to set up the trophies [victory monuments]. So now they have brought us to a position where these enemies of ours, because they are advancing uphill, cannot throw their . . . javelins over [our] heads, while we, with . . . javelins . . . thrown downhill, cannot miss our mark.[51]

Such divine favoritism was not seen to come free; rather, it was thought that the gods expected something in return. In the Athenian view, the gods would provide a certain minimum level of good fortune, prosperity,

and safety as long as the people were pious; that is, as long as they upheld their oaths, made the proper sacrifices, faithfully celebrated the traditional religious festivals, and consulted the gods directly, through oracles (priestesses who acted as mediums between gods and men), when unsure about crucial religious matters.

The Greek Gods

These gods whom the Athenians worshiped so regularly and carefully were, overall, the same ones worshiped by all Greeks. The gods and the stories and traditions surrounding them, along with the Greek language, were unifying forces that instilled the idea that all Greeks were, beneath the surface, kinsmen. The major gods were known as "the Olympians" because early traditions claimed they dwelled atop Mt. Olympus (located in the central mainland region of Thessaly), the tallest mountain in Greece.

Among the most important of these deities were Zeus, ruler of the gods, whose symbols were the thunderbolt and the eagle; Zeus's wife, Hera, protector of marriage and children; Poseidon, Zeus's brother and ruler of the seas, whose symbols were the trident, the dolphin, and the horse; Artemis, moon goddess, mistress of wild animals and hunting, and protector of young girls; her male twin, Apollo, god of the sun, music, truth, and healing; Ares, the war god, whose symbols were the spear and the burning torch; and Athena, Zeus's daughter and the goddess of wisdom and war, whose symbols were the owl and the olive tree.

The Greeks believed that these gods had human forms and also human emotions. The gods made mistakes, fought among themselves, and had marriages, love affairs, and children, just as people did; thus, the Greeks did not perceive the gods as holy or morally perfect, as is common in many modern faiths. "The Greek sense of the holy," historian C. M. Bowra suggests, "was based much less on a feeling of the goodness of the gods than on a devout respect for their incorruptible beauty and unfailing strength."[52] The main factor setting the gods apart from humans, then, was the tremendous power these divinities wielded, power that could either provide for and maintain human civilization or utterly destroy it. "Single the race, single of men and gods," sang the fifth-century B.C. Greek poet Pindar. "From a single mother we both draw breath. But a difference of power in everything keeps us apart."[53]

Athens's Patron Deity

While all Greeks held these gods and their general worship in common, individual city-states had their local favorites. Each had a patron deity who was thought to watch over and protect its inhabitants and with whom it strongly identified itself. This tended, along with geography, kinship, and other factors, to act as a unifying force, bringing together rural and urban sectors of the populace as well as the various social classes. As Bowra puts it, "A whole people might feel that it was protected by watchful presences and united in its admiration for them and its sense of belonging to them."[54]

By providing a deity with his or her own house or shelter, Greeks ensured that a divine patron remained close to the community and could watch over and protect its inhabitants. Thus, the Athenians erected several temples dedicated to their patron deity, Athena, the most famous and splendid of which was the Parthenon on the Acropolis. Inside the building's main room (cella) stood the goddess's statue (the cult image), a magnificent creation almost forty feet high and covered with sheets of beaten gold.

Because Athena was actually thought to reside from time to time within this and her other temples, these structures were considered sacred. The temples' surrounding grounds, which typically featured outdoor sacrificial altars and areas for individual or group prayer, were also held as sacred. (To respect the god's privacy, no worship took place inside the building, as it does in modern churches.) A temple and its grounds together made up the god's sacred sanctuary.

Various Images of and Myths About Athena

Athena's cult image in the Parthenon, known as the *Athena Parthenos,* was only one of several manifestations of the goddess. She was believed to have a number of different sides to her character, each of which personified a special talent or physical or mental attribute. In Greek homes, a room where a young woman, ideally a virgin, dwelled before her marriage was often referred to as a *parthenon.* So Athena Parthenos was "Athena the Virgin," an image emphasizing her feminine beauty and the purity of her wisdom. By contrast, Athena Promachos ("Athena the Warrior Champion") and Athena Nike ("Athena the Victor") were images stressing her physical strength, courage, and fearsome fighting skills.[55] Other manifestations of Athena included Hygieia ("Goddess of Health") and Ergane ("the Worker").

The worship of Athena in Athens was an ancient tradition that originated long before the Classic Age. As classicist Brunilde S. Ridgway points out, "Athens and Athena seem inextricably bound by their names, although it is uncertain which came first, the

This reconstruction of the interior of the Parthenon accurately depicts the huge statue of Athena created by the great sculptor Phidias. However, the altar and congregation of people is fanciful, since worship took place outside the temple.

deity or the city. To be sure, both of them go back to prehistoric times."[56] It is not surprising, then, that the classical Athenians inherited a rich collection of popular myths about the goddess and her relationship with Attica and Athens. The seventh-century B.C. Greek poet Hesiod recorded the details of Athena's miraculous birth, a tale familiar to all Greeks:

Zeus first took the goddess Metis as his wife, but later deceived her and swallowed her, for fate had decreed that Metis would conceive children filled with wisdom. And the first of these would be the bright-eyed maiden Athena, who would have strength and wisdom equal to her father's. Metis remained concealed inside of Zeus and eventually conceived Athena, who received from her father the aegis [his majestic and invincible breastplate], with which she surpassed in strength all her brother and sister gods. And Zeus brought her into the world, bearing the aegis and clad in battle armor, from out of his head.[57]

The Superstitious Man

As is true of people in all ages and of all faiths, some classical Athenians were superstitious, especially about matters relating to the gods and religion. In this excerpt from his often humorous collection of character sketches, appropriately titled *Characters*, the fourth-century B.C. philosopher-scientist Theophrastus provides a priceless record of some of the most common folk beliefs of his day.

"The superstitious man is the sort who, when he meets a funeral procession, washes his hands, sprinkles himself with water from a shrine, puts a sprig of laurel in his mouth [all religious purification rituals] and walks around that way all day. If a weasel [associated then with bad luck, as a black cat is today] crosses his path he goes no further until someone passes between them, or he throws three stones over the road. . . . If owls hoot as he passes by, he becomes agitated and says 'mighty Athena!' [since the owl was her mascot] before he goes on. . . . If he ever notices someone at the crossroads wreathed in garlic [it was commonly believed that crossroads were favorite haunts of evil spirits and that garlic protected against such spirits], he goes away, takes a shower, summons priestesses and orders a deluxe purification. . . . If he sees a madman or epileptic, he shudders and spits down at his chest [the ancient Greek equivalent of knocking on wood]."

Another myth described how Athena and Poseidon had a contest to decide which of them would preside over and protect Attica. Poseidon touched the Acropolis with his trident, producing a miraculous saltwater spring. Athena then countered him by causing the first olive tree to sprout from the hill's summit; seeing this, Zeus and the other gods judging the contest declared her the winner. Another tradition held that Athena had sent an olive-wood statue of herself hurtling out of the sky. The spot on which it supposedly landed, near the Acropolis's northern edge, became the site for a succession of temples that housed the sacred statue the *Athena Polias* ("Athena of the City").

Sometime in the sixth century B.C., a large temple dedicated to Athena Polias was built on the Acropolis's north side, on or near the site of the famous Erechtheum temple constructed during the following century's golden age. Scholars remain unsure, but the older temple may have housed the sacred wooden image until the Persians destroyed the building in 480. (The Athenians took the statue with them for safekeeping when they evacuated the city.) When completed in about 406, the Erechtheum became the statue's new home. The name of the temple derived from Erechtheus, a legendary Bronze-Age Athenian king who came to be considered a sort of partner to Athena or custodian of her temples. (Painters and sculptors often pictured him as a serpent guarding the goddess.)

Marchers in the Great Procession

Together, Athena Polias, her wooden statue, and the temple that housed it played a central role in Athens's most important religious festival—the Panathenaea, translated variously as "All the Athenians," or "Rites of All Athenians."

The Panathenaea was very ancient, having originated sometime in the Bronze Age. Two different myths were associated with its establishment, and it continued to commemorate both of them in classical times. One story told how Erechtheus started the festival to honor Athena's victory over a race of mythical giants. In the other story, the hero Theseus completely reorganized the festival after he unified the towns of Attica into a political whole, creating the Athenian state.

The Panathenaea underwent another major reorganization in 566 B.C., and after that it was the city's greatest festival and also a panhellenic, or "all-Greek," event that attracted visitors from many other city-states. Made up of religious ceremonies, feasts, and musical and athletic contests, it was held annually but celebrated with special pomp every fourth year. Most evidence suggests that it took place between the twenty-third and twenty-eighth days of the Athenian month of Hekatombaion (roughly corresponding with July).

The exact order of the festival's various events is still somewhat uncertain. Most scholars believe that it began with a huge, stately procession (parade) that started at the Dipylon gate in the city's northwest wall, proceeded through the Agora, ascended the Acropolis, and halted near (probably between) the Parthenon and the Erechtheum. This time-honored route was called, appropriately, the

These carved horsemen, presumably members of the Panathenaic Procession, are from the north side of the Parthenon's inner (Ionic) frieze. Designed by Phidias, they magnificently capture in unmoving stone impressions of bursting energy and fluid movement.

Panathenaic Way. Probably reflecting the democratic nature of Athens's government, in the fifth century B.C. the marchers represented all social classes and groups, including *metics* (who carried bronze or silver trays filled with cakes and honeycombs) and freedmen (who bore oak branches). Elderly men, chosen for their handsome looks, carried olive branches (earning them the title of *thallophoroi,* or "bearers of green branches"). Soldiers marched in full armor, slaves led the animals that would be sacrificed later, and children bore trays, water jars, and baskets holding utensils that would be used in the sacrifices. "Of particular note" among these children, Sarah Pomeroy observes,

> are the young girls, called *kanephoroi.* . . . [They] were virgins selected from noble families. Their virginity was a potent factor in securing the propitious [beneficial] use of the sacred offerings and sacrificial

instruments carried in their baskets. To prevent the candidate from participating in this event was to cast aspersions on her reputation.[58]

The Presentation of the Robe

These marching girls were only some of the many women who played important roles in this and other Athenian religious rituals. It was exclusively women, for example, who tended to the Panathenaea's principal single element: the *peplos,* Athena Polias's sacred robe. Months before the celebration, the goddess's high priestess (a position held for life and passed through the female line of an aristocratic clan, the Eteoboutadai) began the creation of a new robe by setting the yarn in the loom. (She was assisted by four girls between the ages of seven and eleven, the *arrephoroi,* who lived on the Acropolis for a year while in

Three youths bearing water jars march in the Panathenaic Procession, as shown on the north face of Phidias's Parthenon frieze. A fourth youth (far right) is raising his jar from the ground.

After visiting Athens in the second century A.D., the Greek traveler Pausanias gave this description of the interior of the Erechtheum in his *Guide to Greece*. It is unknown whether the temple and its contents had changed since the Classic Age, some five hundred years before.

"In front of the entrance is an altar of Zeus the Highest. . . . They put [offerings of] sweet-cakes there. . . . As you go in, there are altars of Poseidon . . . and Hephaestos [god of the forge]. . . . The holiest of all the images [inside the temple] . . . is Athena's statue [the olive-wood Athena Polias]. . . . Rumor says it fell from heaven. Whether this is true or not, I shall not argue about it. [The sculptor] Callimachos made a golden lamp for the goddess. They fill this lamp with oil, and then wait [before refilling it] for the same day of the following year, and all that time the oil is enough to feed the lamp, though it shines perpetually night and day. . . . Over the lamp a bronze palm tree climbs to the roof and draws up the smoke."

The east façade of the Erechtheum as it appears today. The great altar of Zeus stood nearby.

special service to the goddess; two or more other maidens, the *ergastinai*, then proceeded to weave the robe.) This garment would eventually be draped around the *Athena Polias* in the Erechtheum, replacing the one made for the prior festival. By the mid-to-late fifth century B.C., the *peplos* appeared in the grand procession as a sail attached to the mast of a miniature ship carried on a wagon. This nautical theme presumably celebrated the recent rise of Athens's great naval empire.

Once they reached their final destination near the Erechtheum, the marchers stopped and lined up to witness a succession of sacred rites. Convincing evidence suggests that the first of these was the presentation of the *peplos* to the goddess, which consisted of a folding ceremony. A surviving section of one of the Parthenon's friezes (bands of sculptures) depicts a man and a boy holding an already-folded mass of cloth that many scholars believe represents Athena's *peplos*. (Following the Panathenaea, a group of women from the Attic clan Praxiergidai took charge of the robe; later, in a ceremony called the Plynteria, which took place on the twenty-fifth of Mounichion, roughly April, they washed and dressed the statue.)

Religious Beliefs, Festivals, and Customs

A modern reconstruction shows the members of the Panathenaic Procession marching by the Parthenon's east façade. Note the miniature ship (bearing the sacred peplos) *to the right of the building.*

Once the sacred robe had been presented to the goddess, a series of animal sacrifices took place at Athena's great altar, located in the open space between the eastern ends of the Parthenon and the Erechtheum. In each Panathenaea, a hundred Athenian cows and many sheep and other animals brought by visitors from other city-states were sacrificed. Conforming to traditions stretching back into the mists of time, each sacrifice consisted of set rituals. First, the worshipers draped flower garlands over the animal, referred to as the victim, as they led it to the altar. Next, a priest or priestess poured water over the altar to purify it and sprinkled barley grains on the victim for the same purpose. Then he or she used a club to stun the animal and a knife to cut its throat, drained the blood into a bowl, and sprinkled some of it on the altar (or over the worshipers). Finally, several priests used axes and knives to slaughter the victim. The bones and organs were wrapped in the fat and burned, generating smoke that, it was believed, rose up to nourish and appease the goddess; meanwhile, the worshipers divided, cooked, and ate the meat. Noted scholar John Boardman offers the following vivid description of this ritual slaughter enacted at the Panathenaea and other Athenian religious celebrations:

One by one . . . the beasts were dragged before the altar, the stunning axe rose and fell, the knives lost their luster beneath a coat of fat and blood. The rock was slippery with blood, the air heavy with the smell of guts and sweat. The slaughter bred excitement, shouting anticipation of the feasts to come, while the black smoke rolled thick and heavy up into the still and shimmering air, a clear signal to Athena that her citizens had paid their due respect. That smoke would rise for hours to come, while the lean meat . . . was carted down to the marketplace for distribution.[59]

Other Athenian Religious Festivals

Of the many other religious festivals and observances celebrated in Attica, many involved processions and all featured public sacrifices similar, if on a smaller scale, to those in the Panathenaea. One of the most important was the Anthesteria, held from the eleventh to thirteenth of the month Anthesterion (roughly February). Honoring the fertility god, Dionysus, it appropriately took place in the season when the first flower blossoms and other signs of coming spring began to appear. On the first day, the so-called Jar-Opening, samples of new wine were tasted and sacrificed as libations (liquid offerings, usually poured over the altar).

The second day of the Anthesteria, called Wine-Jugs, witnessed a procession in which an image of (or perhaps a masked actor portraying) Dionysus rode in a cart. Also on that day it was customary for everyone, including small children, to drink wine. Children, who received gifts including miniature wine jugs and toys on this day, played an important role in the celebration; for, as classical scholar Erika Simon explains, "Childbirth and fertility were inseparable in the Greek mind."[60]

The festival's third day, called Pots, was more somber and ominous. Pots containing boiled vegetables were sacrificed to satisfy and ward off the spirits of the dead, which supposedly roamed about. At the end of the day (and the festival), people customarily shouted, "Go away, you dreaded spirits! The Anthesteria is over!" or words to that effect.

Highlighting September was the renowned festival of the Eleusinian Mysteries, which was dedicated to Demeter, the goddess who oversaw agriculture. The focus of the celebration was an initiation that people underwent to join a cult (in ancient times a sort of religious congregation). Membership was open to all, male or female, free or slave. New initiates first purified themselves by bathing in the sea and then sacrificed a young pig. After that they joined the other members in a

A restoration of the inner gate of Demeter's temple at Eleusis, in northwestern Attica, site of the renowned Eleusinian Mysteries.

great procession in which sacred objects (stored in the Eleusinion, a temple near the foot of the Acropolis) were carried to Demeter's sanctuary at Eleusis in northwestern Attica. The nature of these objects, as well as the initiations, were secret, hence the name "Mysteries." The festival's climax occurred in the sanctuary's initiation hall (*telesterion*), where a cult leader apparently revealed the sacred objects.

Other prominent Attic festivals included the female-only Thesmophoria (held in October in honor of Demeter), a fertility ritual designed to ensure a plentiful harvest of cereal crops; the Bouphonia (held in June), in which grains and a bull were sacrificed to Zeus; and the City Dionysia (held in March), another celebration dedicated to Dionysus, and famous for its dramatic contests. There were also numerous smaller celebrations and individual sacrifices observed throughout the year.[61]

Prayer, Priests, Omens, and Oracles

In addition to processions, sacrifices, gift giving, and other rituals, public celebrations also involved prayers, as did many more private occasions, such as births, marriages, travel departures, and funerals. An Athenian worshiper prayed standing, with his or her hands raised, palm upwards. If the god being addressed dwelt beneath the earth, the worshiper might stretch his or her arms downward or stomp on the ground to get the god's attention. Kneeling in prayer, which is common today, was seen as unworthy of a free person. Also, prayers were usually said aloud unless the worshiper had some special reason to conceal them.

Because any Athenian could pray or perform sacrifice on his or her own, there were no priests in the modern sense of full-time

Views of the Afterlife

Although most Athenians believed in the existence of a soul (psyche), their views of its possible survival in an afterlife varied considerably, as is the case in most modern societies. The Athenians expressed differing beliefs, writes University of Virginia scholar Jon D. Mikalson in *Athenian Popular Religion*, "on such fundamental questions as whether the soul continued to exist [after death], where the souls of the dead resided, whether the souls had perception of the life of the living, and whether the souls encountered rewards and punishments in the afterlife." The most common traditional folk beliefs held that both good and bad souls descended into the underworld (Hades) guided by the god Hermes, in his manifestation as Psychopompos, "Escorter of Souls."

There, wrongdoers suffered various punishments in a ghastly place called Tartaros; more virtuous people, including initiates of the Eleusinian and other mystery cults, and particularly renowned heroes, lived on in Elysium or the Isles of the Blessed, fabled abodes of eternal happiness. However, though such beliefs still existed in the Classic Age, it is uncertain how widely they were accepted. Evidence shows that a number of classical Athenians thought that the soul lived on inside a dead person's grave marker; that it floated into the sky and lived on in moist air; or, as Plato reported in *Phaedo*, that "on the very day of death it may perish and come to an end—immediately on its release from the body . . . vanishing away into nothingness."

The oracle (priestess) at the Temple of Apollo at Delphi (in central Greece) swoons in preparation for her delivery of a divine message, while eager religious pilgrims look on.

spiritual guides. When family members prayed together at their home altars, the head of the household led the ritual; in larger public ceremonies, a clan or tribal leader or a leading state official usually took charge. In addition, various temples and cults often had part- or full-time staffs of caretakers and specially trained individuals who initiated or aided in sacrifices and other rituals. Any of the people described might bear the title of priest or priestess.

Priestlike individuals were also involved in divination—the reading and interpretation of various kinds of divine signs—an art that required special skills the average person lacked. For example, there was a widespread belief in omens, or signs of impending good

or bad fortune, which might be detected by examining animals' livers, birds' flight formations, and patterns of thunder and lightning. Certain events in dreams were also believed to foreshadow the future. "The gods know all things," Xenophon states, "and in sacrifices, omens, voices, and dreams they give forewarnings to whomever they wish."[62] To attend to such matters, a clan might have its own priest, who inherited his part-time position from a relative. Some people, including Xenophon, as he himself indicates, also commonly consulted professional soothsayers, usually itinerant (traveling) characters who, for a price, explained the meanings of omens, dreams, and signs revealed in sacrifices. Some soothsayers were considered reliable and reputable, but swindlers who preyed on the gullible were evidently not uncommon. Plato complained of men who knocked on "rich men's doors" and offered to thwart their enemies with "magic arts and incantations forcing heaven . . . to do their will."[63]

Soothsayers also sometimes claimed to be able to interpret oracles. These were messages, almost always vague and open to interpretation, thought to have been given to humans by the gods. (The sacred sites where these messages were given, as well as the priestesses who delivered them, were also called oracles.) Since no oracles existed in Attica, on those occasions when the state thought it necessary to ask for divine guidance, the Athenians sent messengers to the famous ones in Apollo's sanctuary at Delphi (in central Greece) and Zeus's sanctuary at Dodona (in northwestern Greece).

It must be emphasized that at least a few Athenians cared little about oracles, omens, or even the gods themselves. For as Plato asserts, some of his countrymen were atheists, or at least not very devout,[64] a situation not uncommon in modern societies. In fact, it is possible that by the late fourth century B.C. many urban Athenians no longer believed in the literal existence of Zeus and the other gods, even though such persons, out of reverence for tradition, continued to practice the age-old rituals and sacrifices. And it is therefore unclear whether Xenophon meant it literally or figuratively when he remarked: "All things in every place are in the hands of the gods, [and] they equally rule all things."[65]

Popular Athletic Games and Leisure Sports

Like all other Greeks, the Athenians had an intense interest in a wide variety of athletic games and sports. In fact, formal organized sports contests in the modern sense originated in ancient Greece. At least by the early Archaic Age (ca. 800–500 B.C.) and probably a good deal earlier, the Greeks used the word *agon,* meaning contest or struggle, to describe athletic contests (as well as other kinds of contests, such as battles and lawsuits). It was in this period (in 776 B.C. according to tradition) that the first Olympic Games were held in honor of Zeus at Olympia (in the city-state of Elis in the northwestern Peloponnesus, the large peninsula that makes up the southern third of Greece). Held every four years, the Olympics were panhellenic games that drew contestants and spectators from all over the Greek world. Partly because of the popularity and success of the Olympics, athletic competitions became increasingly popular in Athens and other poleis during the seventh and sixth centuries B.C.

Moreover, evidence from Athens shows the emergence in this period of a new concept (which likely existed in some other Greek states as well). This was the *kalokagathia* (from the words *kalos,* meaning "beautiful," and *agathos,* meaning "noble" or "learned"), roughly translating as "the mental (or moral) and physical ideal." It stressed striving for a combination of physical and intellectual (or moral) excellence in order to develop a rounded and complete personality. The con-

cept of *kalokagathia* appears to have been fashionable at first mainly in aristocratic circles, since well-to-do and privileged individuals had more leisure time and money to spend training and competing than had poor citizens. But in Athens at least, the rise of democracy, with its ideals of social equality, and the spread of state-sponsored education for all male citizens in the sixth and early fifth centuries popularized the concept. As Vera Olivova, a scholar of ancient athletics, states, "The originally exclusive aristocratic ideal of *kalokagathia* was realized throughout the structure of Athenian society at the height of Athenian democracy."[66]

Thus, many Athenians came to glorify a keen mind in a strong, athletic body. Just how deeply this notion became ingrained in the popular consciousness is illustrated by a common adage repeated by Herodotus, Plato, and other Athenian writers in describing a backward person: "He can neither read nor swim."[67] Though not every Athenian was mentally and physically equipped to achieve this mental-physical ideal, the fact that so many wanted and tried to achieve it significantly influenced the development of the polis's social customs and institutions. In the Classic Age, the gymnasium, in which patrons received both physical and academic training, was an integral feature of town life, and the athletic games held at the greater Panathenaea every fourth year were eagerly anticipated and renowned throughout all of Greece.

Young athletes train in a local gymnasium for an upcoming festival competition. The two grappling at lower left are in the final stages of a boxing match.

The Panhellenic Games

At first, however, sports contests were likely not a part of the Panathenaea or other Athenian state festivals. During early Archaic times, most, if not all, Athenian athletes were aristocrats who affirmed their distinguished social status by competing either in local contests held by their clans, phratries, and/or tribes, or in the Olympics. The first recorded Athenian victory at Olympia was by the runner Pantacles in 696 B.C. Another noted Athenian victor, Phrynon, who won the *pankration* (a combination of wrestling, boxing, and street fighting) in 636, later became a general.

In time, as athletic competition was democratized in Athens, free male Athenians of all walks of life regularly trained for and competed in the Olympics. (Women and slaves were excluded. However, women were eventually allowed to take part in their own small separate games—the Heraea, honoring the goddess Hera—held at Olympia every four

years. Sixteen Elean women organized this competition, which featured one event, a footrace of about 175 yards [160 meters], with separate heats for different age groups). Every four years the men who had trained long and hard eagerly awaited the arrival of the Truce-Bearers, three heralds from Elis who visited every Greek state to announce the exact date of the coming games (which varied from one Olympiad to the next) and to invite all to attend. The heralds also announced the sacred Olympic truce, or *ekecheiria*. For the duration of the truce, originally a month and later extended to three months, all participating states were forbidden from making war or imposing death penalties. This was to ensure safe passage for the thousands of competitors, spectators, and religious pilgrims who attended the games.

Athenians also competed in other panhellenic games, three of which had emerged as near rivals to the Olympics by the sixth century. These were the Pythian Games (honoring Apollo), held at the sacred shrine at Delphi in the third year after each Olympics; the Isthmian Games (honoring Poseidon), staged every two years at a sanctuary on the Isthmus of Corinth, the narrow land bridge connecting southern and central Greece; and the Nemean Games (honoring Zeus), held at two-year intervals at Nemea, a few miles south of Corinth. Together, these "big four" games made up the prestigious *periodos*, or "circuit." Although the city-states saw themselves as tiny separate nations, these events, like the Greek language and the worship of the Olympian gods, served to bind all Greeks. "The sites of the four main games," Olivova writes,

became focal points for the whole Greek world. Amid the fertile variety of the city-states, free of pressure from any central power, it was here that a sense of national identity arose in a purely natural and spontaneous way, through awareness of a high level of shared culture both intellectual and physical, and through a sense of superiority over the slaves and over the neighboring barbarians [non-Greeks]. The outward symbol of this superiority was a strong, tanned, well-developed naked body. It became an ideal for all Greeks, distinguishing them from other peoples, and an object of admiration at all panhellenic festivals.[68]

Spectators cheer on the runners in the hoplitodromos *(race in armor).*
At Athens, the race was two stades (about 1,200 feet) in length, but was considerably longer at Plataea, a small polis on Attica's northern border.

The circuit games featured footraces of various lengths (but no marathon, which developed in modern times[69]); the javelin and discus throws and a running broad jump; wrestling, boxing, and *pankration;* and horse races for riders and chariots.

The Rewards of Winning

As part of his sixth-century B.C. reforms, Solon introduced monetary rewards for panhellenic winners to encourage Athenian athletes to win such events and thereby bring honor and glory to Athens.[70] (The only prize directly awarded at Olympia was a crown of leaves.) Returning home, an Athenian Olympic victor received five hundred drachmas; while a winner at the Isthmian Games received one hundred. Over time, other prizes in addition to such cash awards became common for winners of both foreign games and the local Panathenaic competitions. Among such prizes were valuable bronze tripods, ornamental cups, and jars of olive oil, which the athletes could sell for a profit.

These awards were quite substantial. In the late fifth century, for example, a winning runner at the Panathenaic games received one hundred amphoras (jars) of olive oil. According to noted scholar David Young, "The cheapest recorded price for olive oil in classical antiquity is twelve drachmas an amphora. . . . Thus, twelve drachmas per amphora is the *lowest* usable figure, and we must estimate the value of the . . . victor's prize at a *minimum* of 1,200 drachmas."[71] Evidence shows that the average Greek worker earned about one drachma per day (about three hundred drachmas per year) in the late fifth century. This means that an athlete could receive the equivalent of four years' salary by winning a single footrace! "He could buy six or seven *medium*-priced slaves," says Young, "or a flock of about 100 sheep. Or he could purchase outright two or three houses in Athens."[72]

In addition, it became a custom in Athens to award native sons who had been victorious in the circuit games free meals (a practice called *sitesis*) for life. According to a surviving inscription, "All those who have won the athletic event at the Olympic, Pythian, Isthmian, or Nemean Games shall have the right to eat free of charge in the city hall and also have

Conditions at Olympia

When Athenians traveled to Olympia either as participants or spectators, they made up only a small contingent in a huge assemblage of Greeks from scores and often hundreds of different poleis. The thousands of people and animals raised a lot of dust, and the temperature in August, when the games took place, averaged close to ninety degrees Fahrenheit. This descriptive passage by the first-century A.D. philosopher Epictetus, found in *Discourses,* gives some idea of the uncomfortable conditions and also suggests why so many people were willing to put up with them.

"Some unpleasant and hard things happen in life. And do they not happen at the Olympics? Do you not swelter [in the heat]? Are you not cramped and crowded? Do you not bathe with discomfort? Are you not drenched whenever it rains? Do you not have your fill of tumult [disorder], shouting, and other annoyances? But I fancy that you bear and endure all this by balancing it off against the memorable character of the spectacles."

This nineteenth-century reconstruction of the north section of the Parthenon's Ionic frieze inaccurately depicts a judge crowning a chariot driver. More recent scholarship suggests that the man is a marshal in the Panathenaic Procession who is signaling for the driver to stop so as to avoid running into the marchers ahead.

other honors in addition to the free meals."[73] Among the "other honors" mentioned was the practice of glorifying the most successful athletes almost as gods; poets composed odes about them, and sculptors immortalized them in stone.

The Panathenaic Footraces

Winners at the Panathenaic games received their share of glory, too. Not long after Solon's reforms, the Athenians reorganized the Panathenaea festival (566 B.C.) and added athletic contests that, throughout most of the Classic Age, were held in the Agora.[74] During that period and well after, they were the most prestigious local games held by any Greek state, only slightly lower in stature than the circuit games. In Attica itself, these large-scale, state-sponsored (civic) games honoring Athena came to overshadow the local tribal competitions, which no doubt continued to be staged. In fact, some of the local contests were duly incorporated into the new festival games. University of Texas scholar Donald Kyle comments on the meaning and importance of these new games to contemporary Athenians:

The combination of athletic competitions with a regularly scheduled religious festival enhanced the popularity of both elements. . . . Panathenaic athletics were *civic* as well as *sacred,* and the harmony of these aspects is central to the significance of these games for the Athenians. Ancient Athens did not know our modern separation of church and state: the origins, history, prizes, program, administration . . . all reveal the sacred and civic nature of Panathenaic athletics. As an integral part of the greatest of the Athenian festivals, these athletics . . . were never divorced from the worship of Athena. . . . However, the city itself—and therefore the civic dimension of the games—expanded as the city grew from a troubled sixth-century community into the democratic center of a powerful fifth-century empire. . . . Increasingly the spectacle . . . performed the function of communicating the greatness of Athens to its citizens and to visitors.[75]

An examination of the Panathenaic contests identifies the sporting events that were most popular among Athenians in the Classic Age. At the festival, these events fell into two broad categories, the first being the events that were also held in the circuit and most other panhellenic games; in most cases these were open to non-Athenians as well as Athenians.

As was the case at Olympia, among the most prestigious events in the Athenian games were the footraces. The staples were the *stade*, a sprint of about six hundred feet (a distance itself known as a *stade*);[76] the *diaulos,* a two-*stade* run; and the *dolichos,* a longer run of about twenty to twenty-four *stades*. Archaeological evidence shows that the racecourse in the Agora was wide enough to accommodate only about ten runners at a time; thus initial heats were likely held for each race, with the winners competing in the final contest for the prizes. There was also a *stade* for boys (under eighteen), although apparently no boys' version of the *diaulos* or *dolichos* (which the Olympic program also lacked).

Another important Panathenaic footrace was the race in armor, the *hoplitodromos,* which took its name from *hoplite,* the term describing a heavily armored infantry soldier. (The race first appeared on the Olympic program in 520 B.C. but was almost certainly held earlier in Athens and other

The restored Panathenaic Stadium in Athens, which occupies the exact site of the original. In 1895, a Greek businessman donated four million drachmas to refurbish the facility for the first modern Olympic games.

poleis.) The runners wore a bronze helmet and greaves (lower-leg protectors) and carried a bronze shield, or *hoplon* (actually a wooden disk coated with bronze). Some evidence suggests that over time the helmet and greaves were eliminated, leaving only the burden of the shield. At Athens, the race seems to have been two *stades* in length (and therefore equivalent to the *diaulos*).[77] The *hoplitodromos,* with its armored men clanking along, sometimes bumping into and falling over one another, must have been viewed humorously at times. This is shown in Aristophanes' play *Birds,* in which he poked fun at a group of characters dressed in feathered outfits by likening them to racing hoplites.[78]

Combat Sports, the Pentathlon, and Equestrian Events

Besides the footraces, among the most popular of the other panhellenic contests held in the Panathenaic games were the combat, or "heavy," events. These included wrestling, boxing, and *pankration.* In many ways the *pankration* resembled modern professional wrestling (except that it was not staged entertainment in which the fighters know beforehand who is going to win). Punching, kicking, throwing, pressure locks, and strangling were all allowed, with only biting and eye-gouging forbidden. During a match, which ended only when one fighter surrendered, lost consciousness, or died, judges stood by with rods, ready to deliver painful whacks to rule breakers.

Another popular event, the pentathlon, was a grueling test of overall athletic prowess consisting of five events. Two of these, the *stade* and wrestling, were also held separately of course; but the other three—the javelin and discus throws and the running broad jump—appeared only in the pentathlon. Although the exact sequence of these events is uncertain, scholars generally agree that wrestling came last.

There were also equestrian races, which in general remained dominated by aristocrats even at the height of Athens's democracy. This was because breeding and racing horses required land and wealth. In these events, including a race for solo horses ridden by jockeys and contests for two- and four-horse chariots, Professor Kyle explains,

> the owner of the horse(s), who was not necessarily the driver or rider, claimed the victory; the owner did not personally have to face the danger of riding bareback without stirrups [which, along with the saddle, had not yet been invented] or of steering a light chariot through tight, congested turns.[79]

Indeed, crashes and spills in the frantic eight-mile-long four-horse chariot contest (the *tethrippon*) were probably fairly routine. This excerpt from Sophocles' play *Electra,* which scholars consider accurate, depicts an exciting series of collisions:

> To begin with, all went well with every chariot. Then the Aenian's tough colts took the bit in their teeth and on the turn from the sixth to the seventh lap, ran head-on into the African. The accident led to other upsets and collisions, till the field . . . was a sea of wrecked and capsized chariots. The Athenian driver had seen what was coming and was clever enough to draw aside and bide his time while the oncoming wave crashed into inextricable confusion. Orestes was driving past, purposely holding his team back and pinning his faith to the final spurt; and

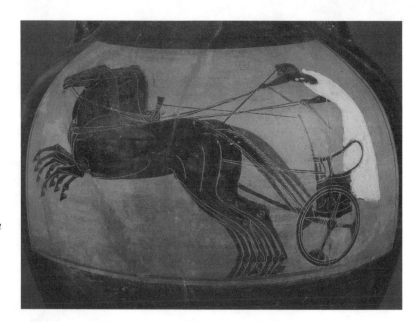

A *black-figured painting on a sixth-century* B.C. *amphora (jar) depicts a four-horse chariot race* (tethrippon). *Serious crashes, spills, and injuries were common in such contests.*

now, seeing only one rival left in, with an exultant shout to his swift horses he drove hard ahead and the two teams raced neck and neck, now one now the other gaining a lead. . . . But at the last [lap], Orestes misjudged the turn, slackened his left rein before the horse was safely round the bend, and so fouled the [turning] post. The hub was smashed across, and he was hurled over the rail entangled in the severed reins, and as he fell his horses ran wild across the course.[80]

Another equestrian event held in the Panathenaic games was neither on the Olympic nor other circuit programs. The *apobates,* or chariot-dismounting race, featured hoplites (pictured on vases either in full armor or nude with helmet and shield) riding chariots. Some scholars think that these athletes (*apobatai,* or "dismounters") jumped off their chariots partway through the race and ran the rest of the distance on foot; others suggest that they continually mounted and dismounted throughout the race.

The Tribal Contests

The second major category of Panathenaic contests included the events that were open only to Athenian citizens. Among these were some military-style equestrian events not held in the circuit games. In one of these events, which appears to have been a "procession" for two-horse chariots, the teams may have been judged on their precision marching and drilling performances. Another event, in which a rider on a moving horse threw a javelin at a target, tested a skill originally developed for warfare.

The other Athenians-only events were the tribal contests, which were larger and more prestigious versions of those long held locally by single tribes and/or their respective phratries and clans. One popular event was the Pyrrhic dance, which tradition held was first performed by Athena directly after her birth from Zeus's head. Painted and sculpted depictions suggest that a tribal team of several men, carrying spears and shields (and often nude), went through a complex and vigorous series of precision moves in unison. According to Plato,

The warrior dance . . . rightly termed Pyrrhic ["fiery"] . . . imitates the modes of avoiding blows and missiles by dropping or giving way, or springing aside, or rising up or falling down; also . . . the imitation of archery and the hurling of javelins, and all sorts of blows.[81]

The tribal events also included various torch races, both team and individual. The Panathenaic team event was a relay race in which members of a tribal contingent of some forty runners passed a lit torch to one another, each running a leg of about two hundred feet (so that the total distance covered was just over a mile and a half). Pausanias describes a solo torch race held in Athens in his own day (second century A.D.) that was probably similar to earlier versions. The contestants, he says, ran into the city from an altar dedicated to Prometheus, the legendary god who gave fire to humans. "The contest consists of running while keeping the torch alight; if the first man's torch is out he loses and the second man wins; if his is not burning either, the third man wins;

if all the torches are out no one wins."[82] If there was indeed a winner, he was honored by having his torch light the festival's sacrificial altar.[83]

Gyms and Leisure Sports

Not surprisingly, the extreme popularity of athletic competitions among Athenians of all social classes made physical training a widespread activity. In combination with the notion of *kalokagathia*, the Athenians also promoted the idea of regular exercise (*gymnastiki*) for good health and a rounded personality. Thus, facilities for training and exercise, the gymnasia (from the term *gymnos*, meaning "naked," since the athletes often trained and competed in the nude), became prominent features in Athenian life. A typical gymnasium consisted of a building with rooms for changing, bathing, and socializing; an adjacent field for practicing various sports; and, in keeping with the physical-mental ideal, some small libraries, reading rooms, and/or lecture halls dedicated to higher learning.

A rare surviving carved representation of the Pyrrhic, or "warrior," dance. The nude participants swung their shields to and fro while executing complex footwork, all in precise unison.

Another place Athenians exercised was the *palaestra*, which was devoted to wrestling (*pale*). It consisted either of a section of a larger gymnasium or a separate facility. The popularity of wrestling among Athenian (as well as other Greek) males cannot be overstated. Under the watchful eye of the *paidotribes*, or athletic instructors, wrestling training constituted the most important part of physical education for Athenian boys. Boys and young men often wrestled informally, much as their modern counterparts play friendly games of football and baseball. Athenian society expected that an accomplished male adult would enjoy and participate in wrestling as much as he would reading or discussing politics with his friends. In his *Symposium*, Plato describes the philosopher Socrates, an intellectual character of slight physical stature, casually going to the gym and wrestling with a much younger man.[84]

Depending on whether they were training for competition or just sparring for exercise or fun, a *palaestra*'s patrons practiced either "upright" or "ground" wrestling. Both styles began with the wrestlers in a standing position. The difference was that in upright wrestling, the only version allowed in formal competitions, the main object was to throw one's opponent to the ground. This constituted a fall (as opposed to modern amateur wrestling, in which holding an opponent's shoulders to the mat gains a fall). Three falls were required for a victory. In the less formal ground wrestling, by contrast, after a successful throw the wrestlers continued to grapple on the ground until one acknowledged defeat (the signal for which was an upraised hand).

Besides wrestling, other leisure sports activities included playing ball (including *episkyros*, a team sport that perhaps resembled modern rugby), fishing, boating, and swimming. Numerous literary references attesting to the swimming prowess of Athenians and other Greeks have survived. One of the most famous from the Classic Age is Herodotus's partial explanation of why Greek casualties in the great sea battle of Salamis (fought against the Persians in 480 B.C.) were so low: "Most of the Greeks could swim, and those who lost

A Greek Gym

In his *On Architecture*, the first-century B.C. Roman architect Vitruvius left behind this description of a Greek gymnasium of his time, which he refers to as a *palaestra*.

"To have a *palaestra* you must build a peristyle [an open space surrounded by rows of columns] . . . which will furnish a walk around it of two *stades*, a distance which the Greeks call a *diaulos*. Three sides of this peristyle should have a portico [roofed area] with a single row of columns, but the south side should be two rows deep, so that when the wind blows in bad weather the rain will not drive in. . . . There should be large sitting rooms, in which philosophers, professors, and others who are intellectually inclined may sit and discourse. . . . [There] should be a room with punching bags . . . a room for washing in cold water . . . a room for athletes to oil themselves . . . a hot room [sauna] . . . and a warm bath. . . . Outside there should be . . . running tracks. . . . [A track] should be not less than 12 feet wide. In this way those who are walking . . . fully dressed will not be bothered by the oiled athletes who are running."

This detail on a cup dated to ca. 520 B.C. shows two young wrestlers (or pankrationists) sparring. Greek athletes competed fiercely, for in their minds winning was all-important and losing a disgrace.

their ships . . . swam over to [the island of] Salamis. Most of the enemy, on the other hand, being unable to swim, were drowned."[85]

Hunting was also popular, especially among members of the upper classes who could best afford horses and packs of hunting hounds. Common game included wild boars, bears, foxes, deer, rabbits, and birds. What was uncommon, however, was for women to go hunting with their husbands; but apparently it did happen on occasion, for in his treatise on hunting, Xenophon writes: "All men who have loved hunting have been good; and not men only, but those women also to whom the goddess [Artemis] has given this blessing [i.e., love of the chase]."[86] This is one of the few Athenian references from the Classic Age hinting at female participation in sporting activities. It may be that evidence for more extensive participation by women will someday be found, but it is more likely that sports remained, like politics, a male-dominated sphere in Athens.

Creative Expression Through the Visual Arts

As the surviving remnants of the Parthenon, Erechtheum, and other monuments of the Acropolis complex attest, Athens produced some of the greatest architecture and art in human history during the Classic Age. These works owed their inspiration and political backing largely to the statesman Pericles (ca. 495–429 B.C.), whom historian Christian Meier calls "a man of extraordinary judgment, imagination, farsightedness, inner independence, and intellectual discipline."[87] What better way to demonstrate that Athens was the marvel of Greece, Pericles asked his countrymen, than by celebrating and honoring Athena, whose divine patronage was instrumental in the city's rise to greatness? Building new, grand, and beautiful temples to her would ensure her continued protection, he proposed. At the same time, a new and magnificent Acropolis complex would be the ultimate symbol of Athenian imperial greatness. As Plutarch would later write, this ambitious project was seen, both at the time and by posterity, as Pericles' and Athens's greatest achievement:

> There was one measure above all which at once gave the greatest pleasure to the Athenians, adorned their city and created amazement among the rest of mankind, and which is today the sole testimony that the tales of the ancient power and glory of Greece are no mere fables. By this I mean his construction of temples and public buildings.[88]

Yet as marvelous as this achievement was, it represented only a small part of Athens's creative-artistic output during the fifth and fourth centuries. Although the sculptor Phidias, the architect Ictinus, and Pericles himself deserve high praise, they did not raise the Parthenon all by themselves. Athens's artistic triumphs, scholar George Wilcoxon reminds us,

> were not all on the Acropolis; some were not even in the city. Nor were all of them sponsored by Pericles. . . . [His efforts] would have come to little had there not been a vast array of talent to set at work. . . . Athenians, like their Greek brethren everywhere, were essentially individualists, and it was this surprising diversity of individual talent that created a wealth of beauty for Athens.[89]

Enhancing this Greek spirit of individualism was the fact that in the Classic Age Athens had a direct democracy in which the people enjoyed personal freedoms unprecedented in the ancient world. These freedoms included the right to express oneself not only politically but creatively as well, especially in the visual arts, which included architecture, sculpture, painting, and theater.

This does not mean that every Athenian was a creative genius. Phidias, Ictinus, and Sophocles were no more average or typical Athenians than architect Frank Lloyd Wright, playwright Eugene O'Neill, and filmmaker Orson Welles were average or typical Americans. But the works of all of these talented individuals touched the lives of their respective countrymen and helped to define the identities and characters of their respective societies. The latent energies of Athenian builders, artists, writers, and craftsmen were encouraged and often lavishly funded by the state or by private citizens. At the same time, their works kept many Athenians employed, entertained, and/or spiritually fulfilled.

Construction Projects and Workers

Because of their imposing size and visual splendor, and also because so many people labored to construct them, the public buildings erected in Athens constitute the most obvious example of the community's collective creative expression. The most productive single period for such construction projects was the second half of the fifth century B.C. These few decades witnessed the undertaking not only of the Acropolis complex—including the Parthenon, Erechtheum, Temple of Athena Nike, and Propylaea (the massive entrance gate)—but also the Temple of Hephaestos (god of the forge) and other public buildings in the Agora; the Temple of Ares at Acharnae, about seven miles north of Athens; the Temple of Poseidon located at Sounion on Attica's southern tip; and the Temple of Nemesis (daughter of Night[90]) at Rhamnous on Attica's northeastern coast.

Thousands of Athenians, free and slave, citizen and *metic*, worked side by side on these projects, which required a wide variety of skills to complete. The most comprehensive description of the various kinds of workers involved in such a project is from Plutarch's biography of Pericles, which lists the occupations of those who toiled to raise the Parthenon:

The materials to be used were stone, bronze, ivory, gold, ebony, and cypresswood, while the arts or trades which

The stately ruins of the Parthenon, perhaps the most architecturally perfect building ever erected, loom above the Acropolis's battlements in this view from the southwest.

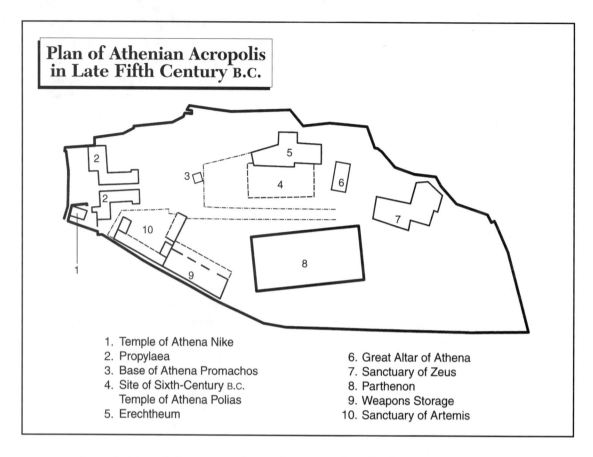

Plan of Athenian Acropolis in Late Fifth Century B.C.

1. Temple of Athena Nike
2. Propylaea
3. Base of Athena Promachos
4. Site of Sixth-Century B.C. Temple of Athena Polias
5. Erechtheum
6. Great Altar of Athena
7. Sanctuary of Zeus
8. Parthenon
9. Weapons Storage
10. Sanctuary of Artemis

wrought or fashioned them were those of carpenter, modeler, coppersmith, stonemason, dyer, worker in gold and ivory, painter, embroiderer, and engraver, and besides these the carriers and suppliers of the materials, such as merchants, sailors, and pilots for the sea-borne traffic, and wagon-makers, trainers of draft-animals, and drivers for everything that came by land. There were also rope-makers, weavers, leatherworkers, road-builders, and miners. Each individual craft, like a general with an army under his separate command, had its own corps of unskilled laborers at its disposal . . . [and consequently] the city's prosperity was extended far and wide and shared among every age and condition in Athens.[91]

Methods for Raising Stone Buildings

An examination of some of the steps involved in erecting such a large structure reveals much about the occupations and construction methods of ancient Greece. The first step was to cut and transport the thousands of stone blocks needed for the building's walls and columns. To separate the stones from the exposed slice of mountainside in a quarry, the masons first used mallets and chisels to cut grooves in the stone mass. Next, they drove wooden wedges into the grooves and saturated them with water. As the wedges absorbed the water, they expanded, forcing the stone to crack, after which the workers used crowbars and other tools to finish freeing the stones. Gangs of men then used levers, ropes, and pulleys to nudge the stones onto wooden sleds, after which, using more ropes, they painstakingly maneuvered the sleds down the hillside. Once onto flat ground, the workers transferred the stones to wagons, which carried them to the work site.

At the site, teams of masons prepared the still rough and unfinished stone blocks. Using mallets and flat chisels, they cut each block to fit in a spot that had been premeasured by one of the foremen. Such work had to be extremely precise since, as a rule, Greek builders did not use mortar in temples and other large structures. Instead, they trimmed the stones to fit together snugly and then joined one to another with I-shaped iron clamps. First, they chiseled rectangular slots in the top surfaces of the two blocks to be joined; then, they inserted the clamps and poured melted lead into the spaces that remained, making sure that when the lead dried its surface was even with those of the stones. When the next course was laid on top, its stones conveniently covered and hid the clamps in the course below. (The Parthenon and many other ancient buildings still bear unsightly pockmarks where scavengers in later ages chiseled out the clamps to sell the metal.)

Meanwhile, another group of masons prepared the stones for the temple's columns. These rounded pieces were called drums. A typical column in a temple colonnade consisted of about eleven separate drums, one stacked on top of another, with a decorative top piece—the capital—stacked atop the uppermost drum. To cut a drum to the desired diameter, a mason placed one of the still rough and somewhat irregular stone disks on top of a circular stone pattern already prepared on the ground. Using a mallet and a pointed metal tool, appropriately called a "point," he carefully chipped away pieces of the disk until its diameter matched that of the pattern below it. Like the wall blocks, the column drums were joined by fasteners, each of which was hidden by the drum stacked above it.

Because the drums were enormously heavy (between five and ten tons each), lifting them was a tremendous challenge. The builders met this challenge by employing simple but effective mechanical hoists. The most

Projects Aimed at Eliminating Unemployment

In this excerpt from his *Life of Pericles*, Plutarch tells how Pericles proposed to use surplus money to employ Athenians in projects for the benefit of the whole community and thereby maintain the city's greatness.

"'Once completed, [Athens's public works] will bring her glory for all time, and while they are being built will convert that surplus to immediate use. In this way all kinds of enterprises and demands will be created which will provide inspiration for every art, find employment for every hand, and transform the whole people into wage-earners, so that the city will decorate and maintain herself at the same time from her own resources.' [Pericles] was also anxious that the unskilled masses, who had no military training, should not be debarred from benefiting from the national income, and yet should not be paid for sitting about and doing nothing. So he boldly laid before the people proposals for immense public works and plans for buildings, which would involve many different arts and industries and require long periods to complete."

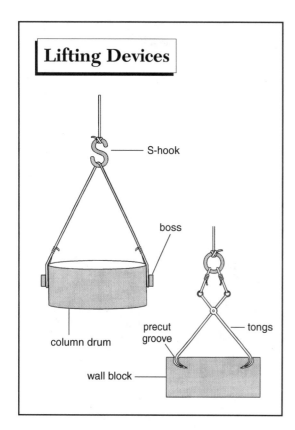

S-hook

boss

column drum

precut groove

tongs

wall block

common type consisted of a derrick (a wooden framework with ropes and pulleys attached to one of its horizontal beams), which was firmly planted on the ground. One rope led away from the derrick and over a wooden scaffolding beam placed directly above the spot where the builders wanted a stone to sit. They attached the stone to the hoist either by looping a rope around bosses (knobs) that had been left protruding from the stone for this very purpose or with a set of metal lifting claws, called the grapple or tongs. After hoisting the stone and setting it in place, workers used crowbars to adjust its position more accurately and then removed the bosses, if any.

Sculptors' Tools and Techniques

Once the basic structural elements of a building were in place, the sculptors and painters went to work. A temple usually had statues,

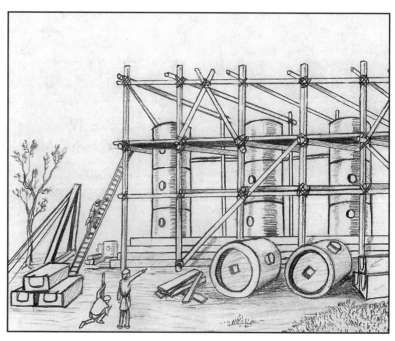

This drawing of an early stage of temple construction shows how the scaffolding encases the half-finished columns. The bosses protruding from the column drums will be removed later.

The Citizenry Captured in Stone

The Parthenon's inner frieze depicted a two-part parade of humans, horses, and chariots that a number of scholars believe depicts the Panathenaic procession. This description of the frieze's surviving sculptures is by the British Museum's Ian Jenkins and is excerpted from his book *The Parthenon Frieze.*

"The two branches of the frieze present a procession composed of various groups of figures arranged in a sequence. On the [building's] west side we see horsemen, some paired, others shown singly. The directional flow is from right to left, or south to north. . . . The long north side carries forward the cavalcade begun on the west, and the horsemen occupy nearly half of the total number of slabs. Ahead of them come chariots, then groups of figures walking in procession, including elders, musicians, pitcher-bearers, tray-bearers and figures leading cattle and sheep as sacrificial victims. Turning the corner onto the east side we find . . . a procession of girls carrying vessels . . . [and] male figures leaning on staves [walking sticks] and engaged in conversation. . . . Ahead of them are shown the gods, whose seated pose allows them to appear larger than the mortal figures in the frieze. . . . The southern branch of the frieze follows a pattern similar to that of the north. The two processions do not actually meet, since the gods are placed between them."

life-size or larger, in its pediments (the triangular gables on its front and back) and sculpted reliefs (or sometimes paintings) in its frieze (ornamental band running around the perimeter just above the colonnade). Other buildings featured decorative sculptures and/ or paintings. The Agora's Stoa Poikile, erected in the 460s B.C., for instance, had several large painted murals (the most famous of which depicted the Battle of Marathon and the sack of Troy, by the artists Micon and Polygnotus, respectively). Many freestanding statues—of gods, military heroes, winning athletes, and so on—adorned the religious sanctuaries and other parts of the city.

To create such statues, sculptors often set up temporary workshops near the site to minimize the risk of damage when moving the finished works. The first step was to make clay models, often full-size ones, supported by wooden or metal frames. Guided by a master sculptor, apprentices completed the models based on his design; after the master had given his approval, the apprentices roughed in the broad proportions in the marble versions. The master finally took over, providing the details and finishing touches. He would work "quite swiftly," says historian John Boardman,

with the sharp iron point that brought off large marble flakes. Then the . . . claw chisel, which safely gouged broad swathes on the stone, then the flat chisel, and rasps and rubbers to smooth away the tool marks. Where dress fell in deep, shallow-catching folds, or there was deep cutting to be attempted between the legs of horses . . . then the bow drill was brought out. An assistant spun the shaft, and rows of close-set holes were drilled straight into the surface to define masses which could be safely broken away, leaving the chisel to finish the folds of drapery, or intricacies of anatomy.[92]

After the sculptors finished carving the figures, other craftsmen took over. Metalworkers attached precast bronze spears, horse harnesses, and other details to holes the sculptors had drilled in the appropriate places. Then, painters applied wax and bright colors, bringing the statues to life. They used the wax to polish the surfaces representing flesh, producing the look of suntanned skin.

In the years immediately preceding the Classic Age, one of the most popular subjects for sculptors was the kouros, *or "youth," usually carved to honor the god Apollo.*

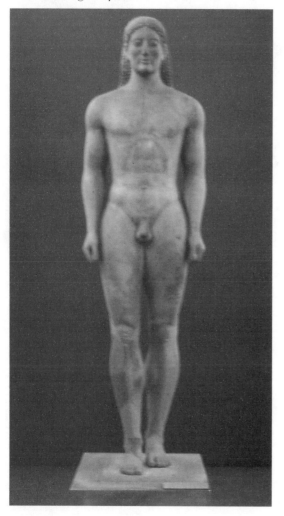

They then painted the hair, lips, and eyebrows a deep red and the clothes and other trappings various shades of red, blue, and yellow. (The painters also applied liberal coats of bright colors, especially reds and blues, to various outer sections of temples and other large structures. These colors faded and wore away over many centuries, leaving the stark, off-white stone façades familiar today.)

The Potter's Art

A more refined mode of painting was integral to the production of pottery, one of Athens's chief industries. Using hands-on techniques inherited from artisans of prior centuries, the master potters and their assistants molded wet *ceramos* ("potter's clay") on wheels and fired it in kilns reaching a temperature of one thousand degrees Fahrenheit. They crafted their wares for practical use, yet they strove for originality of design and excellence of execution in every piece. According to Thomas Craven, an authority on ancient art, their wares

> were part and parcel of the routine life of the people. Vases were designed to hold flowers and fruits, or as decanters for wine, or as storage jars. Beautiful cups were fashioned for drinking purposes and all sorts of table china were decorated with religious scenes. The ceremonials in the temples and at . . . altars necessitated a great variety of sacred vessels; the holy olive oil given as a prize in the Panathenaic games required a container of impeccable artistry, as did those of other festivities such as a special form of amphora, with a long neck, which held the water for the bridal bath—and was also used as a monument for those who died

unmarried. The exquisitely shaped *lekythus,* a bell-mouthed, narrow-necked, single-handed vase, was filled with fragrant oils and buried with the dead or left at the graveside.[93]

In the century preceding the Classic Age, most such vases, amphorae, and other vessels utilized the "black-figure" decorative style pioneered by Athenian artisans, including Sophilos, the first potter known to have signed his work. In this style, figures of men were painted in black on the natural buff-colored background of a fired pot. The artist then used a pointed tool to etch details into the figures. Black-figure pottery reached its height of popularity between 550 and 525 B.C. in the work of an unnamed artisan whom scholars refer to as the Amasis Painter.

Not long afterward a new style, the "red-figure," appeared. In a reversal of the older style, red-figure technique left the figures of humans and animals in the fired pot's natural reddish tone and rendered the backgrounds

This beautiful black-figured amphora, made in Attica during the Classic Age, shows artisans at work in a boot-maker's shop.

A Goddess Sculpted in Ivory and Gold

One of the most magnificent sculptures created in the Classic Age was Phidias's *Athena Parthenos,* which stood inside the Parthenon. Although the huge statue has not survived, a few miniature copies made later, along with the following description by Pausanias in his *Guide to Greece,* allude to the statue's grandeur. Pausanias witnessed the statue firsthand and gives some idea of its appearance.

"In the temple which they call the Parthenon . . . the cult image itself is made of ivory and gold. In the middle of her helmet there is placed the image of a sphinx . . . and on each side of the helmet griffins are represented. . . . Griffins are beasts which look like lions but have the wings and beak of an eagle. . . . The statue of Athena stands upright and wears a tunic that reaches to the feet, and on her breast [on the aegis] the head of Medusa [a mythical monster], made of ivory, is represented. In one hand she [Athena] holds a figure of [the goddess] Victory about four cubits [six feet] high and in the other she holds a spear; at her feet is placed a shield, and near the shield is a serpent. This serpent would be Erechtheus."

black. This allowed for the application of more realistic details, which were applied with a brush (although etching was still employed for certain fine details). Red-figure pottery was perfected in the early 400s B.C. by such Athenian artisans as the so-called Berlin Painter, who excelled at portraying human limbs and muscles.[94]

Athens Invents the Theater

The theater was another visual art that involved, affected, and benefited a large proportion of the Athenian populace. In fact, this unique combination of art form and public entertainment, which millions of people in many lands have enjoyed over the centuries, originated in Athens in the sixth century B.C. Its subsequent development was rapid and spectacular. In less than a century, a series of informal songs and speeches recited by worshipers in roadside religious processions evolved into formal dramatic competitions held in large public facilities.[95] Almost all of the theatrical concepts familiar today, including tragedy, comedy, acting, directing, costumes, scenery, and even theater tickets and acting awards, were invented in Athens in the early Classic Age.

The dramatic competitions were part of the City Dionysia, the religious festival held in March in honor of the fertility god Dionysus. (Such competitions were also presented on a smaller scale at the Rural Dionysia, held in December, and the Lenaea; also dedicated to Dionysus, held in January.) As in the Panathenaea, a splendid procession of thousands of people wound its way along Attic roads, in this case ending in the urban center's theater. The first Athenian theater was erected perhaps in the early 530s. Its exact location and physical layout are unknown. Evidence suggests that it was in the Agora and that it consisted of a circular "dancing place," or orchestra, where the actors performed; a central altar (*thymele*), for sacrificing to Dionysus; and an audience area (*theatron*) with wooden bleachers. In about 499, these bleachers collapsed in the middle of a performance, killing many of the spectators.

After this unfortunate incident, the Athenians constructed the Theater of Dionysus against the southeastern base of the Acropolis. In its initial form, the theater featured an orchestra eighty-five feet in diameter. To avoid another disaster, the seating, which could accommodate up to fourteen thousand spectators, consisted of wooden planking covering earthen tiers carved into the hillside. (In a fourth-century B.C. renovation, the wooden seats were replaced by stone versions.) A rectangular structure called the *skene,* or "scene building," was erected behind the orchestra and facing the audience. The *skene* provided a background for the actors and also housed dressing rooms and perhaps a storage area for stage props.

Contests and Audiences

After the City Dionysia's great procession reached the theater, a bull was sacrificed to Dionysus and the contests began. Over the course of a few days, several playwrights presented their works, which in the first several decades were exclusively tragedies. The stories came mostly from mythology and explored the relationship between humans and gods as well as basic human emotions and social and moral themes of interest to all. When comedy was introduced in the early fifth century B.C., it provided audiences with an emotional release and relief from the grimness of the tragic presentations. The comic plays also

The remains of the Theater of Dionysus, located along the southeastern rim of the Acropolis's base. Frequently remodeled and expanded, by the mid–fourth century B.C. the facility held an estimated 14,000 spectators.

became an important outlet for political expression by poking fun, often with unheard-of candor, at institutions, leaders, and other citizens. "In no other place or age," comments noted scholar Victor Ehrenberg, "were men of all classes attacked and ridiculed in public and by name with such freedom. . . . The ultimate reason for this . . . was the fact that comedy was an internal affair of the sovereign people as a whole, and so there was complete *parrhesia*, freedom of speech."[96]

Indeed, Athenian audiences felt free to express themselves in ways that would be considered rude or disruptive in modern theaters. As historian of ancient theater James H. Butler puts it,

They were caught up in a feverish excitement, an intense interest in the outcome of the various contests. Their volatility and enthusiasm were more characteristic of present-day football and baseball spectators. . . . The hundreds directly competing for prizes and honors in the City Dionysia sharpened the appetite for victory. Add to this group several hundred, perhaps several thousand, former chorus members . . . performers, flute players, and extras sprinkled among the audience. They had competed in previous festivals and were quite knowledgeable on the finer points and techniques of performance. Refreshments to sustain the "dawn to dusk" audience were hawked [sold by roving vendors], thereby increasing the general noise and commotion.[97]

Admission for these spectators was free at first; however, increasing demand for seats soon necessitated the introduction of tickets (in about 450 B.C. by Pericles). By the mid–fourth century, a seat for the day cost two obols (about one-quarter of an average worker's daily wage). The tokens looked similar to coins and were made of bronze, lead, ivory, bone, or terra-cotta.

Having watched all of the plays, the spectators remained seated to witness the festival's most eagerly anticipated moment: the awards ceremony. A panel of ten judges issued lists that rated the works of participants in four categories: tragic playwrights, comic playwrights, leading tragic actors, and leading comic actors. The winner in each category received crowns of ivy similar to those awarded to Olympic victors.

Patrons of the Arts

These expensively staged theatrical competitions were financially supported by a system of public contributions called liturgies (*leitourgiai*, or "the people's burdens"). The government required the well-to-do members of the community to pay for theatrical productions, erecting statues and monuments, distributing food at religious festivals, backing the singers and dancers who performed at many festivals, and other such services; each year the names of new arts patrons were chosen, in rotation, from lists of better-off citizens.

The backer of a play was called a *choregus*. In the fifth century B.C., he could expect to spend an average of three hundred to fifteen hundred drachmas to mount one play; but some *choregoi* spent three thousand drachmas (enough to sustain a small family for several years) or even more. Most *choregoi* took pride

Dramas of Surpassing Power and Beauty

In this excerpt from his edition of Aeschylus's only surviving trilogy, the *Oresteia*, published as *The Orestes Plays of Aeschylus*, noted translator Paul Roche summarizes the major themes of fifth-century B.C. Greek tragedy.

"[They came] principally from the old stories of the gods and heroes as handed down by oral and written tradition in epic and lyric poetry, particularly from the *Iliad* and *Odyssey* of Homer. Homer became a kind of bible-*cum*-history of the ancient world, and a compendium of its values. Occasionally a drama was built upon contemporary history, as in *The Persians* of Aeschylus. . . . [Theater] never quite lost its religious

motive and impetus . . . [and maintained] a powerful moral and ethical sense which sought not only to inspire but to teach. . . . Man's ways with . . . the gods—and vice-versa—are explored . . . side by side with the ever-important and always bewildering questions of destiny, freedom, personal responsibility, and sin. . . . [Also presented are] man's ways with man: honor, justice, retribution, law, liberty, duty; and his universal emotions: love, hate, revenge, fear, pride, pity, and regret. These are the themes and emotions that pulse through the stories taken by [Athenian playwrights] . . . and turned into dramas of surpassing power, significance, and beauty."

This modern restoration shows what the Theater of Dionysus probably looked like in the second century B.C., during the Hellenistic Age, when Greek independence was giving way to the might of Rome.

in this duty, partly because it could bring them considerable prestige. In a speech delivered in court, one former patron bragged:

> I won first prize at the Thargelia [a festival of Apollo held in May] with a men's chorus, having spent 2,000 drachmas. In the archonship of Glaukippus [410 B.C.] I spent 8,000 drachmas on Pyrrhic dancers at the Great Panathenaea, and I won first prize as *choregus* with a men's chorus at the Dionysia, spending 5,000 drachmas.[98]

The result of such subsidies was that wealth—like the talents that designed Athens's temples and sculptures—though always concentrated in the hands of a few individuals, often benefited all members of society.

CHAPTER 6

The Wages of War on Land and at Sea

As important as politics, religious worship, athletics, and the arts were in Athenian life, none of these was more important than, or could have existed at all without, the services of the state's citizen soldiers. Before, during, and after the Classic Age, wars in Greece were frequent. And throughout the Classic Age itself, Athens was at war fully three-quarters of the time! Occasionally the Athenians fought non-Greek invaders, as when the Persians entered Greece in 490 B.C. and again in 480. Usually, however, the foes were other Greek states, and the wars and battles were most often waged to assert political dominance rather than to gain territory. During the fifth century, for example, Athens frequently used its considerable military might to coerce and punish rebellious members of its maritime empire.

In light of the reality that warfare was a regular condition of life, Athens's part-time militiamen had to be ready almost at a moment's notice to grab their weapons and march off to fight. This partly explains the widespread popularity of athletics and regular exercise. A man who failed to keep himself physically fit increased his chances of dying on the battlefield; likewise, if enough men were out of shape, it could spell defeat and ruin for the entire polis. Whether Athenian males served in the army or the navy, they had a crucial responsibility to defend the community, including its traditions, institutions, and honor, at all costs; and they did not take this responsibility lightly.

High levels of patriotism and earnestness did not necessarily guarantee success, however, as illustrated by the Athenian land army's rather dismal record of wins and losses. In fact, with the notable exception of their spectacular victory over the Persians at Marathon in 490, the Athenians rarely won a major land battle on their own.[99] This was largely because Athens, like most other Greek states, could not afford to train, equip, and pay a large standing army. Instead, the state had to rely on part-timers who supplied their own armor and weapons and received only two years of formal training. By contrast, Athens's archenemy, Sparta, had a small but full-time standing army whose soldiers underwent many years of grueling training; not surprisingly, it was the most feared and consistently successful land army in Greece until the mid–fourth century (when the Theban army finally defeated it).

Yet Athens made up for its shortcomings as a land power with its navy, which was long the supreme force in Greece. Because of the demands of their naval empire, which reached its peak in the late fifth century, the Athenians were constantly at sea and gained tremendous naval expertise (as opposed to most other Greek states whose navies were small and had only limited training and experience; Sparta had no naval war fleets until the end of the fifth century). This situation prompted Thucydides' famous description of the two Greek superpowers at the opening (in 431) of the disastrous Peloponnesian War:

At the head of one [coalition of states] stood Athens, at the head of the other Sparta, one the first naval, the other the first military power in Greece. . . . The whole period from the Persian war to this, with some peaceful intervals, was spent by each power in war, either with its rival, or with its own revolted allies, and consequently afforded them constant practice in military matters, and that experience which is learned in the school of danger.[100]

Training

The exact role an Athenian fighting man played in this "school of danger" often depended on his economic condition. The fact that the state did not fully provide arms and other military necessities meant that each soldier had to arm himself with whatever he could afford. Only the wealthy could afford to keep and train horses, for instance, so they made up the bulk of the cavalry (an auxiliary force that never numbered more than about twelve hundred in the Classic Age). The armor and weapons used by the infantrymen, or the hoplites, were not cheap either, and these men therefore came mainly from the middle and upper classes. (A young man whose hoplite father had been killed in battle was armed at public expense.) The poorest citizens, often referred to as the *thetes*, typically served either as lightly armed (i.e., unarmored) auxiliary troops or more often as rowers in the navy.

The hoplites, who made up the core of the land army and who were also the principal

The Athenians (aided by their allies the Plataeans) drive the Persians back to their ships at Marathon, a stunning victory that for a time gained Athens the image of Greece's savior.

fighters on the decks of warships, received the most extensive training. At the age of eighteen, an Athenian hoplite recruit entered a military training corps called the Epheboi. A recruit, or *ephebe,* swore this patriotic oath:

> I will not shame the sacred arms, nor will I abandon my comrade wherever I am stationed. I will fight for the defense of the sacred rites both divine and human, and I shall not leave my country diminished when I die, but greater and more powerful, as far as I am able and with the help of all. I will obey the magistrates ruling in their wisdom, and the established laws and any others which the magistrates in their wisdom may establish in the future. If any person seeks to overthrow them, I will oppose him as far as I am able and with the help of all. I will honor the ancestral sacred rites.[101]

During the first half of their two years of service, the *epheboi* underwent training in the use of weapons and in battlefield tactics; in the second year, they patrolled Attica's outlying frontiers. From the time they graduated from the corps at age twenty until they reached age sixty, these hoplites remained liable for military call-up (although men over fifty, like those under twenty, mainly guarded Attica's borders and only rarely fought).

A Hoplite's Panoply

The armor, weapons, and battle formations and tactics utilized by Athenian hoplites were part of a mode of warfare that had become widespread in Greece by the beginning of the seventh century B.C. Hoplite warfare was a disciplined, highly specialized system that relied to a great extent on the panoply, or extensive and heavy array of arms and armor, wielded by each participant. For this reason, hoplites were designated as *heavy infantry,* a common term in Western warfare ever since.

The basic element of a hoplite's panoply consisted of his shield, the *hoplon* (or *aspis*), which dictated his fighting style and from

A hoplite, seen in full battle gear (left) and also in an "at ease" posture, without helmet and greaves. The cuirass shown is a linothorax, *comprised of layers of linen.*

Athenian Hoplites Suffer a Defeat

This excerpt from Thucydides' *The Peloponnesian War* vividly describes the Athenians' defeat by the Boeotians (Thebans) at the Battle of Delium in the winter of 424 B.C. (the seventh year of the war). Mentioned are many standard battle procedures, including the paean, general's speech, running charge, *othismos* (shoving match), and erection of a victory trophy.

"On the side of the Athenians, the hoplites throughout the whole army formed eight [ranks] deep, being in numbers equal to the enemy. . . . The armies being now in line and upon the point of engaging, Hippocrates, the general, passed along the Athenian ranks, and encouraged them. . . . [He] had got half way through the army with his exhortation [pep talk], when the Boeotians . . . struck up the paean, and came against them from the hill; the Athe-nians advancing to meet them, and closing at a run. . . . [The armies] engaged with the utmost obstinacy [i.e., pushed against each other], shield against shield. The Boeotian left, as far as the center, was worsted by the Athenians. . . . Some of the Athenians also fell into confusion in surrounding the enemy and mistook and so killed each other. . . . [On] the right, the Thebans . . . got the better of the Athenians and shoved them further and further back. . . . At length in both parts of the field . . . with their line broken by the advancing Thebans, the whole Athenian army took to flight. Some made for Delium and the sea . . . others for Mount Parnes, or wherever they had hopes of safety, pursued and cut down by the Boeotians. . . . The Boeotians set up a trophy, took up their own dead, and stripped those of the enemy."

whose name the term *hoplite* may have derived (it may also have come from the term *hopla,* meaning "heavy gear"). The average *hoplon* was about three feet in diameter and weighed roughly seventeen to eighteen pounds. It was gently concave with a wooden core reinforced on the outside by a coating of bronze (although sometimes by layers of ox hide). The inside was lined with leather and featured a distinctive gripping system. This consisted of a bronze strip with a loop, the *porpax,* in the middle, through which the hoplite passed his left forearm; and a leather handle, the *antilabe,* which he grasped with his left hand. This system allowed the man to let go of the handle and hold a spare weapon in his left hand without losing his shield; it also helped to relieve the burden of the shield's considerable weight.[102] Vase paintings show that sometimes a leather curtain hung down from the shield's bottom rim to protect the hoplite's legs against arrows and other missiles.

A hoplite's torso was protected by a breastplate called a cuirass. According to John Warry, an authority on ancient warfare,

The most expensive type was the muscled cuirass made of bronze, but the most common type of protection was a cuirass made up of numerous layers of linen or canvas glued together to form a stiff shirt (*linothorax*). These were often reinforced with metal plates or scales. This [largely] replaced the earlier bronze bell type [by the late sixth century B.C.]. The cuirass

A late-fourth-century B.C. *painting on terra-cotta depicts a lightly armored hoplite running, presumably at an enemy.*

bronze shin guards called greaves, which were often molded in the shape of leg muscles (usually exaggerated). He applied them by pulling them open and then clipping them on, in the manner of modern wrist and ear cuffs.

The hoplite's panoply was completed by his weapons, the principal one being a thrusting spear about seven feet long. It had an iron head and also a sharp butt spike in case the head broke off. The hoplite also carried an iron sword about two feet long (in a scabbard of wood covered by leather), a backup weapon used primarily when the spear was lost or broken.

Because this combination of arms and armor was so heavy and cumbersome, a hoplite usually donned it only shortly before battle. Whenever possible, he had a servant accom-

The ridge atop this "Thracian"-style helmet, popular in the late Classic Age and early Hellenistic Age, originally supported a colorful horsehair crest.

itself consisted of a body piece with arm holes cut out and the bottom cut into two layers of "feathers" (*pteruges*). This wrapped around the body and was laced together on the left-hand side, where the join was protected by the shield. A yoke which bent down over the shoulders and tied to the chest completed the cuirass.[103]

The panoply had other protective features, including a bronze helmet. The most popular type of helmet in the late Archaic Age and on into the Classic Age was the Corinthian, which had eye slits and breathing spaces for the nose and mouth. There were many variations, some with cutouts for the ears (since it was otherwise difficult to hear when wearing a helmet), some with movable visors or cheek pieces, and others topped by decorative plumes of horsehair. A hoplite also wore

pany him to carry the panoply and help him get into it. During a blockade of an enemy town in 428, Thucydides mentions Athenian hoplites each receiving pay of two drachmas a day, one for himself and one for his servant.[104] A servant also received one-half the food ration allotted to a hoplite.[105] When on the march, an army without such servants was at a serious disadvantage, as illustrated by Thucydides' description of Athenian hoplites fleeing an army of Syracusans and Spartans in 413:

> Dejection and self-condemnation were . . . rife among them. . . . The whole multitude on the march [was] not less than forty thousand men. All carried anything they could which might be of use, and the hoplites . . . contrary to their custom while under arms, carried their own provisions, in some cases for lack of servants,

in others through not trusting them, as they [the servants] had long been deserting and now did so in greater numbers than ever.[106]

The Phalanx

The armored hoplites fought in a special formation called the phalanx, a long block of soldiers several ranks deep. A depth of eight ranks was most common, but on occasion there might be more than eight or as few as three or four ranks. At Marathon, for example, the Athenian commander thinned the center of his battle line to four or fewer ranks to make that line match the mile-wide front of the larger Persian army (to ensure that the enemy would not outflank, or move around and behind, his own army).

A Terrible Din of Smashed Bronze and Dying Men

In this excerpt from *The Western Way of War*, an informative study of hoplite warfare, noted classical scholar Victor D. Hanson provides this evocative description of the sounds of battle. These must have haunted the participants, for several ancient writers mentioned them.

"The entire noise of men and equipment was concentrated onto the small area of the ancient battlefield—itself usually a small plain encircled by mountains, which only improved the acoustics [magnified the sounds]. . . . The *nature* of the sound also changed from that of recognizable human speech—the war cry or song . . . to a terrible cacophony [din] of smashed bronze, wood, and flesh. . . . The Greeks recognized that the peculiar noise of this initial crash came

from a variety of sources. First, there was the dull thud of bronze against wood as either the metal spear point made its way through the wood core of a hoplite shield, or as soldiers struck their shields against the bronze breastplates and helmets of the enemy, or as wooden shield was bashed into shield. . . . The live sounds were more animal-like than human: the concerted groans of men exerting themselves, pushing forward in group effort with their bodies and shields against the immovable armor of the enemy. . . . Finally . . . there were all too often the noises of human misery. Here arose a tortured symphony of shrieks as a man went down with a wound to the groin, the steady sobbing of a soldier in extremis [dying], a final gasp of fright as the spear thrust found its way home."

By the beginning of the Classic Age, the Athenian phalanx consisted of ten divisions (*taxeis*), each with its own commander (*taxiarchos*). Each division was drawn from one of the ten tribes organized by Cleisthenes. It broke down into several subdivisions called *lochoi*, each *lochos* perhaps consisting of one hundred men and supervised by a junior officer (*lochagos*).[107]

The *taxiarchoi* and most other officers fought in the front rank, as did the *strategoi*, the generals to whom these officers reported. (Although Athens had ten *strategoi*, only three customarily accompanied the army on a campaign. One of the three was chosen as permanent commander in chief or perhaps they rotated that position from day to day.) There may also have been a few "rear rankers" (*ouragoi*), veteran officers who stood behind the formation and made sure that the men in the rear ranks were doing their jobs.

The traditional phalanx was an extremely effective offensive unit in its heyday (ca. 700–350 B.C.) for two reasons. First, it afforded its members a high degree of protection. When assembled in open order, soldiers stood about five to six feet apart; in close order, the mode most often adopted when closing with an enemy, soldiers stood perhaps two to three feet apart and their uplifted shields created a formidable unbroken protective barrier. The other factor that made the phalanx so formidable was its tremendous and lethal forward momentum. As the formation made contact with the enemy lines, the hoplites in the front rank jabbed their spears at their opponents; at the same time, the hoplites in the rear ranks pushed at their comrades' backs, pressing

A phalanx in action, in this case against the Persians (left) in the Battle of Plataea, in 479 B.C. The phalanx remained the most lethal offensive unit in Mediterranean warfare for over 400 years.

them forward at the enemy. This maneuver was known as the *othismos*, "the shoving."

For all of these reasons, as the second-century B.C. Greek historian Polybius remarked, "So long as the phalanx retains its characteristic form and strength, nothing can withstand its charge or resist it face to face."[108] This was particularly true against non-Greeks. At the height of the battle at Marathon, for instance, the Athenian wings, constituting small twin phalanxes, turned inward on the Persian center, and, like living steamrollers, annihilated all in their path. Likewise, at Cunaxa (in Persia) in 401, the Persians were so frightened of the approaching phalanx that they simply ran away. Xenophon, who served in the Greek ranks that day, later recalled that

> the two lines were hardly six or seven hundred yards apart when the Greeks began to chant the battle hymn and moved against the enemy. . . . Then altogether [they] broke into a ringing cheer, "Eleleu, eleleu!" and all charged at the double. . . . They also beat the spears on the shields to scare the horses. Before one shot reached them, the barbarians turned and fled. At once the Greeks pursued with might and main. . . . Not one Greek was hurt in this battle, except one on the left wing, said to have been shot by an arrow.[109]

The "battle hymn" (paean) and "cheer" (war cry) to which Xenophon refers are among various standard battle procedures undertaken by Athenian and other Greek hoplites. These rituals, which occurred in fairly rapid succession, included sacrificing a goat or other animal just prior to battle to determine if the religious signs were favorable; listening to a spirit-raising speech by the commanding general; singing the paean to steel their nerves and intimidate the enemy; breaking into a running charge when coming within range of enemy archers; screaming the war cry during the charge; engaging in the *othismos;* and, if they were victorious, erecting on the battlefield a trophy (*tropaion*), a wooden framework displaying captured enemy arms, to give thanks to the gods.

Cavalry and Light-Armed Troops

The Athenians made little use of cavalry in the Classic Age. In fact, during the Persian Wars of the early fifth century B.C. the Athenians and their Greek allies appear not to have employed horsemen at all. As noted military historian Peter Connolly suggests,

> The Greeks can hardly have been unaware of the effect that the Persian cavalry must have on them. Perhaps they were relying on Thessaly and Boeotia [Greek regions known for raising horses] to provide contingents of horsemen to keep the Persian cavalry busy. When these areas fell to the Persians, the southern states did not try to compensate for this. When they won in spite of it, they probably convinced themselves that they did not need cavalry.[110]

Only in the late fifth century, during the Peloponnesian War, did cavalry come into common use. Even then it was not employed in large-scale shock action (direct charges on the infantry). Horses were not plentiful in Attica or most other parts of southern Greece. Similarly, saddles and stirrups had not yet been invented, so riders had difficulty staying on swiftly moving horses, a problem that would have been greatly magnified if the riders had worn armor. Like other Greeks in

Here, from his *Hellenica*, Xenophon describes the defeat of a group of some six hundred Spartan hoplites by *peltasts* commanded by the Athenian general Iphicrates outside the walls of the Greek city of Corinth in 390 B.C.

"Iphicrates . . . saw that the Spartans were neither in great force nor protected by peltasts or cavalry, and came to the conclusion that it would be safe to attack them with [his] own peltasts. If they marched along the road, they could be shot at with javelins on their unprotected side and mowed down; and if they tried to pursue their attackers, it would be perfectly easy for the peltasts, light and fast on their feet, to keep out of the way of the hoplites. . . . Iphicrates with his peltasts attacked the regiment of Spartans. And now as the javelins were hurled at them, some of the Spartans were killed and some wounded. . . . The polemarch [Spartan commander] then ordered the infantry in the age groups 20 to 30 to charge and drive off their attackers. However, they were hoplites pursuing peltasts at a distance of a javelin's throw, and they failed to catch anyone. . . . When the Spartans . . . turned back from the pursuit, Iphicrates' men wheeled round, some hurling their javelins again from in front while others ran up along the flank, shooting at the side [of the Spartan formation] unprotected by the shields. . . . Then, as things were going very badly, the polemarch ordered another pursuit. . . . But in falling back from this pursuit even more men were killed than before. . . . The Spartans were already at their wits' end . . . and now when, in addition to all this, they saw hoplites [from the city] bearing down on them, they broke and ran. . . . In all the fighting and in the flight about two hundred and fifty of them were killed."

A cavalryman chases down and dispatches an escaping warrior in this fourth-century B.C. bas-relief.

this period, the Athenians used their cavalry mainly to protect the phalanx against enemy skirmishers (javelin throwers and archers), to chase down escaping enemy hoplites after the phalanxes had fought, and to rescue their own injured or escaping hoplites. Regarding a cavalryman's weapons, Xenophon advocated that he carry two javelins. "For the skillful man," he wrote,

> may throw the one and can use the other in front or on either side or behind. They are also stronger than the spear and easier to manage. We recommend [the horseman] throwing the javelin at the longest range possible. For this gives a man more time to turn his horse and to grasp the other javelin.[111]

Light-armed troops, or skirmishers, included archers, slingers, and *peltasts (peltastai*, who got their name from their characteristic small round or crescent-shaped shield, the *pelta*). *Peltasts* carried small bundles of javelins; their chief tactic was to approach the enemy, throw their weapons, and then run away. As in the case of horsemen, Athens made little use of light-armed troops until the late fifth century. Most skirmishers were mercenaries (hired soldiers); the archers were imported from the large Greek island of Crete; the slingers were recruited from another Greek island, Rhodes; and the *peltasts* hailed from the northern Aegean region of Thrace. In 390 an Athenian general named Iphicrates used a highly trained group of Thracian *peltasts* to defeat a small force of Spartan hoplites. After that battle, Athens and other Greek states increased their use of these skirmishers; Athens even began recruiting *peltasts* from its poorer classes to supplement the mercenaries it continued to import.

The Athenian Navy

After the close of the Persian Wars, Athens helped organize the Delian League, a confederacy of over a hundred Greek poleis whose principal aim was to protect Greece from further Persian attacks. Deftly utilizing their large fleet, the Athenians swiftly gained almost complete mastery of the Aegean sea-lanes and turned the league into their own maritime empire. By about 420 B.C., Athens had at least 350 warships, far more than any other Greek state. It maintained its naval supremacy until its defeat at the conclusion of the Peloponnesian War (in 404), after which the victorious Spartans confiscated all but twelve of Athens's vessels.

These vessels were mostly triremes, the most common Greek warship from the late sixth century on. A trireme was generally about 130 feet long, 18 feet wide, and featured three banks of oars, sixty-two in the upper bank (*thranite*), and fifty-four each in the middle and lower banks (*zygite* and *thalamite*). The ship carried a total crew of about 200 men. This included 170 rowers, who were not slaves but highly trained professionals recruited mainly from Athens's lower classes (although some were likely mercenaries). The crew also included a flute player who kept time for the rowers, a fighting force of 10 (on occasion up to 40) hoplite marines (*epibatai*) and 4 archers, and 15 deckhands. One of the latter, the helmsman (*kubernetes*), was usually more experienced and knowledgeable about naval matters than anyone else on board.

The captain, or trierarch (*trierarchos*), was most often a wealthy individual fulfilling his duty to the state. Each year, as part of Athens's system of public liturgies, a few hundred wealthy men were each called on to outfit and maintain one trireme for the coming season. The state provided the ship and paid the rowers; while the trierarch supplied much of the equipment, paid the officers, bore the cost of any repairs, and commanded the ship (although if a novice he probably heavily relied on the advice of the veteran helmsman).[112]

Such warships were impractical for long-term naval strategy because they could not remain at sea for long periods. This was mainly because they lacked eating and sleeping facilities, which meant that they had to be beached at least once a day. Describing the tactics of an Athenian admiral, Xenophon writes,

> When his force [of ships] was just ready to take the morning or evening meal, he

would order the leading ships of the column to come about . . . and form into line . . . facing the land, and at a signal make them race to the shore. And it was something really to be proud of to be the first to get water or whatever else was wanted and to be the first to get one's meal.[113]

Naval strategy was therefore of a short-term nature, mainly concerned with winning an individual battle. The tactics were fairly simple. Most often, a warship, which was outfitted with a bronze "beak" on its prow, tried to ram an opposing ship. One common maneuver was first to attack at an angle and sheer off the enemy's oars, leaving that side of the hull open to ramming. Another tactic was to use grappling hooks or ropes to lock two ships together; the hoplites from one vessel then boarded the other and fought in hand-to-hand combat.

Athens in Decline

These same naval tactics, with some minor variations and improvements, prevailed for centuries to come. Shortly after the close of the Classic Age, however, it was no longer Athenian or even Greek ships that dominated the Mediterranean seaways. The Greeks, who never learned to get along and could not unite into a single, powerful state, eventually fell prey to the growing might of Rome, master of the Italian peninsula. In the second and first centuries B.C. the Romans made Attica and other parts of Greece part of their expanding empire.

The unusually wide, two-masted trireme depicted in this restoration is a transport ship. Triremes designed for battle were typically narrower and single-masted.

Persian galleys flounder in the Battle of Salamis (480 B.C.), in which the Athenian navy played a pivotal role. Thereafter, Athens retained naval supremacy for almost eight decades.

Under Roman rule, Athens retained many of its local customs and festivals, and daily life went on much as before; but the city never again possessed the great power and prestige it had in the fifth century. Nor did it enjoy its independence again until modern times. Moreover, with the end of Athenian democracy, that enlightened form of government virtually disappeared from the earth until the eighteenth century, when the American Revolution revived it in a new form.

But though Rome ended Athenian political rule, it fortunately preserved much Athenian culture. The highly practical Romans, who often adopted the best aspects of the peoples they conquered, were greatly influenced by Greek, and especially Athenian, customs, arts, and ideas. In literature, architecture, painting, law, religion, philosophy, and other areas, the Romans incorporated Greek styles and concepts, creating the Greco-Roman cultural fusion that eventually came to be called "classical." Later, many centuries after Rome's fall, the modern world rediscovered classical culture, so much of which was based on Athenian models. In this way, Athenian democratic concepts, architectural wonders, and other cultural ideals came profoundly to shape the modern Western world. And Pericles' bold prophecy—that future ages would stand in awe of his city and its achievements—in the fullness of time became a reality.

Notes

Introduction: Athens, the "School for Greece"

1. *Women in Ancient Greece.* Cambridge, MA: Harvard University Press, 1995, p. 97.
2. Quoted in Thucydides, *The Peloponnesian War,* trans. Rex Warner. New York: Penguin Books, 1972, p. 148.
3. *The Greek Experience.* New York: New American Library, 1957, pp. 199–200.
4. There are several reasons for this lack of evidence for other Greek states. For example, some, like Miletus, Corinth, and Thebes, suffered almost total destruction at the hands of the Persians, Romans, Macedonians, or others, ensuring the loss of most or all local histories, public records, and literature. On the other hand, other states, most notoriously Sparta, produced little literature and/or did not often share what they did produce with other Greeks. As a result, modern histories and cultural studies of ancient Greece must rely mostly on Athenian sources, which may not always render accurate, fair, unbiased views of rival states.
5. Quoted in Xenophon, *Memorabilia and Oeconomicus,* trans. E. C. Marchant. Cambridge, MA: Harvard University Press, 1965, p. 387.
6. Quoted in Sarah B. Pomeroy, *Goddesses, Whores, Wives, and Slaves: Women in Classical Antiquity.* New York: Schocken Books, 1995, p. 92.
7. See, for instance, Ian Jenkins, *The Parthenon Frieze* (Austin: University of Texas Press, 1994) and Jennifer Neils, *Goddess and Polis: The Panathenaic Festival in Ancient Athens* (Princeton, NJ: Princeton University Press, 1992), which discuss various modern interpretations of the Parthenon sculptures and what they reveal about Athenian society and religion.
8. Quoted in Thucydides, *The Peloponnesian War,* published as *The Landmark Thucydides: A Comprehensive Guide to the Peloponnesian War,* trans. Richard Crawley, ed. Robert B. Strassler. New York: Simon and Schuster, 1996, p. 114.
9. Quoted in Thucydides, *The Peloponnesian War,* in *The Landmark Thucydides,* p. 115.

Chapter 1: The Growth of the City-State and Its Government

10. *The Greek Commonwealth: Politics and Economics in Fifth-Century Athens,* rev. ed. New York: Oxford University Press, 1961, pp. 66–67.
11. *Critias,* in *The Dialogues of Plato,* trans. Benjamin Jowett. Chicago: Encyclopaedia Britannica, 1952, p. 480.
12. For a useful short overview of the Mycenaeans and Bronze Age civilization, see Andrew R. Burn, *The Penguin History of Greece* (New York: Penguin Books, 1985, pp. 35–60); a worthwhile, more detailed treatment is William Taylour, *The Mycenaeans* (London: Thames and Hudson, 1985); the fall of Mycenaean civilization is explored in Robert Drews, *The End of the Bronze Age: Changes in Warfare and the Catastrophe of ca. 1200 B.C.* (Princeton, NJ: Princeton University Press, 1993); and modern discoveries and studies of Troy

and the Trojan War are thoroughly covered in Michael Wood's very readable *In Search of the Trojan War* (New York: New American Library, 1985).

13. Quoted in *Life of Solon,* in *The Rise and Fall of Athens: Nine Greek Lives by Plutarch,* trans. Ian Scott-Kilvert. New York: Penguin, 1960, p. 60.

14. *Social Values in Classical Athens.* London: Dent, 1976, p. 5.

15. *Social Values in Classical Athens,* p. 9.

16. These tribes—Geleon, Aegicores, Argades, and Hoples—were named after the sons of Ion, a mythical figure who supposedly settled Athens in the dim past. It appears that this myth, dramatized in Euripides' play *Ion* (written sometime between 418 and 414 B.C.), was an artificial one, invented by Athenians at some unknown date to explain the colonization of the western coast of Asia Minor (now Turkey) by settlers from Athens shortly after the end of the Bronze Age. That region, where many Greek cities were eventually established, subsequently became known as Ionia after Ion.

17. *The Histories,* trans. Aubrey de Sélincourt. New York: Penguin Books, 1972, pp. 364–65.

18. Fisher, *Social Values in Classical Athens,* p. 17.

19. *The Histories,* p. 364.

20. *The Rise of the Greeks.* New York: Macmillan, 1987, p. 69.

21. The term *demos* had other meanings besides the citizen body of the polis; it also referred to the poor citizens (in contrast to the aristocrats), the sum of the state's democratic laws and institutions, democrats (in contrast to those opposed to democracy), and any local district (deme).

22. The number of members needed for a quorum (the legal number required to transact business) is unclear. Some political functions, such as bestowing honorary citizenship or ostracism (deciding whether a leader should be banished), required a quorum of 6,000; it is uncertain whether this held true for all functions. In any case, the quorum may have been smaller in the fifth century than in the fourth.

23. *Everyday Life in Ancient Greece.* Oxford: Clarendon Press, 1968, p. 53.

24. *The Athenians and Their Empire.* Vancouver: University of British Columbia Press, 1987, p. 116.

25. These included the eponymous archon, who dealt with state festivals and family matters; the *polemarch,* originally the commander in chief of the army but as of the 480s a civilian official in charge of lawsuits involving foreigners; the "king" archon, who supervised the community's religious functions; and six "keepers of the law," who oversaw the law courts. Archons served for one year and were not eligible for reelection.

26. *The Athenian Constitution,* trans. H. Rackham. 1952. Reprint, Cambridge, MA: Harvard University Press, 1996, p. 129.

27. *The Athenians and Their Empire,* p. 121.

28. There was usually an odd number of jurors, which prohibited a tie vote; on the rare occasions when a tie occurred, the defendants were automatically acquitted.

29. Quoted in *Aeschylus: Prometheus Bound, the Suppliants, Seven Against Thebes, the Persians,* trans. Philip Vellacott. Baltimore: Penguin Books, 1961, p. 129.

30. *Pericles of Athens and the Birth of Democracy.* New York: Free Press, 1991, p. 10.

31. Quoted in Thucydides, *The Peloponnesian War*, in *The Landmark Thucydides*, p. 113.

32. Kagan, *Pericles of Athens and the Birth of Democracy*, p. 10.

Chapter 2: The Household and the Lives of Its Members

33. *Statesman*, in *The Dialogues of Plato*, p. 581.

34. Quoted in *Memorabilia and Oeconomicus*, p. 415.

35. Quoted in *Memorabilia and Oeconomicus*, pp. 419–23. Some modern scholars suggest that such tracts by Xenophon and other Greek men were cynical attempts to rationalize, reinforce, and perpetuate antifemale sexism and male dominance. For this view, see for instance Eva C. Keuls, *The Reign of the Phallus: Sexual Politics in Ancient Athens* (New York: Harper and Row, 1985), especially pp. 1–11. My view is that Xenophon did succeed in reinforcing the sexist status quo, but not by conscious design; he and most other Athenian men and women believed that status quo to be the natural order of things.

36. *Greek and Roman Life.* Cambridge, MA: Harvard University Press, 1986, p. 5.

37. *Greek and Roman Life,* p. 12.

38. A villa with such a tower, dated to ca. 350–300 B.C., was discovered in the early 1970s near modern Vari, south of Athens.

39. Quoted in Waldo E. Sweet, ed., *Sport and Recreation in Ancient Greece: A Sourcebook with Translations.* New York: Oxford University Press, 1987, p. 203.

40. *The Book of the Great Generals of Foreign Nations*, trans. John Rolfe. Cambridge, MA: Harvard University Press, 1960, p. 371.

41. Quoted in *Memorabilia and Oeconomicus*, pp. 425–27.

42. *Women in Ancient Greece*, pp. 136–37.

43. *Goddesses, Whores, Wives, and Slaves*, p. 63. In cases in which the woman's father had no sons, she could perpetuate the *oikos* in the role of an *epikleros* (literally meaning "without property"). As such, she was expected to marry a male relative on her father's side of the family, one of a traditionally accepted succession of candidates beginning with his brother; the family property then passed, along with her, into his custody.

44. *Women in Ancient Greece*, pp. 122–23.

45. One of the most famous surviving Athenian law court speeches, Lysias's *For Euphiletus* (ca. 400–380 B.C.), deals with just such a situation. Euphiletus slew a man he had caught with his wife, but the man's relatives accused Euphiletus of plotting the whole situation leading up to the killing and prosecuted him on a charge of murder. See Kathleen Freeman, *The Murder of Herodes and Other Trials from the Athenian Law Courts* (New York: W. W. Norton, 1963, pp. 43–53) for a full translation of the speech and some excellent commentary.

46. *Laws*, in *The Dialogues of Plato*, p. 723.

47. The exact reasons for exposure of infants (*ekthesis*) in Athens are unclear. But it is reasonable to assume that, as in other societies that have practiced it, the most commonly rejected babies included those with severe birth defects and unwanted females, although healthy males might on occasion also be exposed if the parents did not want or could not afford to raise any more children.

48. *Children and Childhood in Classical Athens.* Baltimore: Johns Hopkins University Press, 1990, pp. 23–24.

49. *Protagoras*, in *The Dialogues of Plato*, p. 46.

Chapter 3: Religious Beliefs, Festivals, and Customs

50. Quoted in Kenneth J. Atchity, ed., *The Classical Greek Reader.* New York: Oxford University Press, 1996, pp. 218–19.
51. Published as *A History of My Times*, trans. Rex Warner. New York: Penguin Books, 1979, pp. 127–28.
52. *The Greek Experience*, p. 57.
53. *Nemean Odes*, in *The Odes of Pindar*, trans. C. M. Bowra. New York: Penguin Books, 1969, p. 206.
54. *The Greek Experience*, p. 69.
55. In the 450s B.C., Phidias, the sculptor who would later fashion the *Athena Parthenos* and design the Parthenon's sculptures, created a huge bronze statue of Athena Promachos that stood for a time on the Acropolis. It was said that people on ships far out at sea could see sunlight reflecting off the statue's shield and spear.
56. "Images of Athena on the Acropolis," in Neils, *Goddess and Polis*, p. 119.
57. *Theogony*, in Rhoda A. Hendricks, ed. and trans., *Classical Gods and Heroes: Myths as Told by the Ancient Authors.* New York: Morrow Quill, 1974, pp. 38–39.
58. *Goddesses, Whores, Wives, and Slaves*, pp. 75–76.
59. *The Parthenon and Its Sculptures.* Austin: University of Texas Press, 1985, p. 19.
60. *Festivals of Attica: An Archaeological Commentary.* Madison: University of Wisconsin Press, 1983, p. 94.
61. In addition to these religious festivals, there were several secular festivals that featured sacrifices, including the Synoecia, which celebrated Theseus's ancient union of the peoples of Attica; the Democratia (established after Athenian democracy, which had been briefly dismantled, was restored in 403 B.C.), celebrating Athens's democratic institutions; and various local celebrations held by phratries, tribes, and demes.
62. *Cavalry Commander*, in Xenophon, *Scripta Minora*, trans. E. C. Marchant. Cambridge, MA: Harvard University Press, 1993, p. 293.
63. *Republic*, in *The Dialogues of Plato*, pp. 313–14.
64. See *Laws*, in *The Dialogues of Plato*, pp. 787–88.
65. *Anabasis*, trans. W. H. D. Rouse. New York: New American Library, 1959, p. 57.

Chapter 4: Popular Athletic Games and Leisure Sports

66. *Sports and Games in the Ancient World.* New York: St. Martin's Press, 1984, p. 125.
67. See, for instance, Plato's *Laws*, in *The Dialogues of Plato*, p. 670.
68. *Sports and Games in the Ancient World*, p. 120.
69. Contrary to popular belief, the marathon race (a long-distance run of 26 miles, 385 yards), a widely popular sporting event today, did not exist in ancient times. Modern Olympic officials introduced it in 1896 to commemorate the legendary feat of Phidippides, an Athenian soldier and runner. Supposedly, following the 490 B.C. Battle of Marathon in which the Athenians defeated an invading force of Persians, he ran the twenty-five miles or so to Athens, proclaimed the victory, and dropped dead from exhaustion. It remains unclear whether this inspiring

feat actually happened, but there is no doubt that no Greek (or Roman) games ever featured a footrace nearly as long as the marathon.

70. See Plutarch, *Life of Solon*, in *The Rise and Fall of Athens*, p. 65.

71. *The Olympic Myth of Greek Amateur Athletics*. Chicago: Ares, 1984, p. 116.

72. *The Olympic Myth of Greek Amateur Athletics*, p. 127.

73. Quoted in Sweet, *Sport and Recreation in Ancient Greece*, p. 120.

74. A special new stadium was constructed in a ravine east of the Acropolis for the 330 B.C. Panathenaic festival. It was later lavishly refurbished by the Romans; after it was excavated and partially restored in the 1880s, it housed the first modern Olympic Games in 1896.

75. "The Panathenaic Games: Sacred and Civic Athletics," in Neils, *Goddess and Polis*, p. 80.

76. Since an Attic foot measured .328 meters, as compared to .305 meters for a modern English foot, the Athenian *stade* (or *stadion*) was likely closer to 660 feet.

77. By comparison, at Plataea, a small polis north of Athens, the race in armor was fifteen *stades* (almost two miles) long. The Plataean hoplite race became the most famous in the ancient world, even more important than the one at Olympia. This was because Plataea was the site of a huge battle, fought in 479 B.C., in which a united Greek army crushed an invading Persian force, saving Greece.

78. A well-known translation is by R. H. Webb in Moses Hadas, ed., *The Complete Plays of Aristophanes*. New York: Bantam Books, 1962, p. 239.

79. "The Panathenaic Games," in Neils, *Goddess and Polis*, p. 89.

80. *Electra and Other Plays*, trans. E. F. Watling. Baltimore: Penguin Books, 1953, p. 90.

81. *Laws*, in *The Dialogues of Plato*, p. 726.

82. *Guide to Greece*, trans. Peter Levi, vol. 1. New York: Penguin Books, 1971, pp. 88–89.

83. The organizers of the modern Olympic Games borrowed this idea by having a lone runner carry a torch around the stadium and light the symbolic Olympic flame. But no such ceremony, nor any other event involving torches, took place at the ancient Olympics.

84. See *Symposium*, in *The Dialogues of Plato*, p. 170. Although the scene described is a fictitious one designed to illustrate the points Plato is making in the dialogue, the matter-of-fact way he presents it suggests that it would not have been unusual for Socrates to have wrestled in the gym.

85. *The Histories*, p. 553.

86. *On Hunting*, in *Scripta Minora*, p. 457.

Chapter 5: Creative Expression Through the Visual Arts

87. *Athens: Portrait of a City in Its Golden Age*, trans. Robert and Rita Kimber. New York: Henry Holt, 1998, p. 430.

88. Life of Pericles, in *The Rise and Fall of Athens*, p. 177.

89. *Athens Ascendant*. Ames: Iowa State University Press, 1979, p. 217.

90. Nemesis personified the righteous anger of the gods, and her cult at Rhamnous constitutes one of the few examples of Greeks worshiping an abstract quality in the manner of a humanlike deity.

91. *Life of Pericles*, in *The Rise and Fall of Athens*, pp. 178–79.

92. *The Parthenon and Its Sculptures*, p. 33.

93. *The Pocket Book of Greek Art*. New York: Pocket Books, 1950, pp. 95–96.

94. Another Athenian pottery style that gained popularity in the fifth century B.C. was the "white-ground" technique in which figures were painted in delicate lines against a white background. White-ground paintings were most often used on the *lekythoi* placed in burial sites.

95. By the eighth century B.C., the rituals attending worship of the fertility god Dionysus had developed a kind of poetry and ceremony called dithyramb (or "goat-song" because men dressed as satyrs, creatures half-goat and half-man, took part). Telling Dionysus's story, and later those of other gods and heroes, the dithyramb took on increasingly dramatic form until the 530s, when an innovator named Thespis introduced the concept of a worshiper *impersonating* rather than merely telling about the heroes; this concept gave birth to acting and formal theater. See Don Nardo, *Greek and Roman Theater*. San Diego: Lucent Books, 1995, pp. 13–23.

96. *The People of Aristophanes: A Sociology of Old Attic Comedy*. New York: Schocken Books, 1962, p. 26.

97. *The Theater and Drama of Greece and Rome*. San Francisco: Chandler, 1972, p. 69.

98. Lysias, *On a Bribery Charge*, quoted in Joint Association of Classical Teachers, *The World of Athens: An Introduction to Classical Athenian Culture*. New York: Cambridge University Press, 1984, p. 229.

Chapter 6: The Wages of War on Land and at Sea

99. This victory was due mostly to the inferiority of the Persians' armor, weapons, training, and tactics; any Greek infantrymen of that time would likely have defeated them, as evidenced by the fact that the Athenians' only allies in the battle, who fought as well as they, hailed from the tiny and fairly typical polis of Plataea (located on Attica's northern border).

100. *The Peloponnesian War*, in *The Landmark Thucydides*, p. 14.

101. Quoted in Fisher, *Social Values in Classical Athens*, pp. 152–53.

102. In 1973 a group of professors at Pennsylvania State University conducted an experiment that showed just how burdensome these shields, along with other battle gear, could be when a hoplite had to exert himself. They chose ten young physical education majors in top physical condition and attached fifteen pounds of weights to each. Each was also given a nine-pound simulated shield and instructed to hold it upright with his left arm. The young men then began running, as if charging an enemy formation. Not one was able to keep the shield chest-high for more than seventy-five yards, and most were unable to run farther than three hundred yards. One, a varsity long-distance runner, managed to run a mile, but collapsed in a state of total exhaustion. It should be noted that the burdens these students carried were considerably lighter than an ancient hoplite's total panoply. See Walter Donlon and James Thompson, "The Charge at Marathon," *Classical Journal*, vol. 71, 1976, and "The Charge at Marathon Again," *Classical World*, vol. 72, 1979.

103. *Warfare in the Classical World*. Norman: University of Oklahoma Press, 1995, p. 35.

104. See *The Peloponnesian War*, in *The Landmark Thucydides*, pp. 166–67.

105. See *The Peloponnesian War*, in *The Landmark Thucydides*, p. 231.

106. *The Peloponnesian War*, in *The Landmark Thucydides*, p. 471.

107. Most scholars assume that at this time Athens still employed most of the elements of the "archaic *lochos*," the hypothetical basic unit of the early phalanx from which the formation's more complex structure supposedly evolved. For a detailed discussion, see Peter Connolly, *Greece and Rome at War*. London: Greenhill Books, 1998, pp. 37–43.

108. *Histories*, in *Polybius: The Rise of the Roman Empire*, trans. Ian Scott-Kilvert. New York: Penguin Books, 1979, p. 509.

109. *Anabasis*, p. 38.

110. *Greece and Rome at War*, p. 48.

111. *The Art of Horsemanship*, in *Scripta Minora*, p. 363.

112. In the later years of the Peloponnesian War, when Athens found it increasingly difficult to find enough wealthy men of military age to take on this duty, the state resorted to having two men share it. In 340 B.C. the duty was spread further among several men. It was abolished altogether in the late fourth century B.C.

113. *Hellenica*, p. 313.

Glossary

acropolis: "The city's high place"; a hill, usually fortified, central to many Greek towns; when capitalized, the term refers to the Acropolis in Athens.

agathos: "Noble," "learned."

agon: A contest.

agora: A Greek marketplace; when capitalized, the term refers to the Agora in Athens.

amphidromia: A postbirth ceremony in which relatives and friends sent gifts to the newborn's family.

amphora: A jar.

andron: A room in which the master of a house dined and entertained guests.

antilabe: A leather handle on the back of a hoplite's shield that he gripped with his left hand.

apobates: A chariot race in which the driver dismounted one or more times during a race; *apobatai:* dismounters.

archon: A public administrator.

arrephoroi: Athenian maidens who lived on the Acropolis for a year in service to the goddess Athena.

astai: Citizens who lacked political rights (most often applied to women).

atimia: "Dishonor"; loss of citizenship; *atimos:* one who has lost citizenship.

aulos: A flute.

bosses: Knobs left projecting from the sides of stone building blocks; workers attached ropes to the bosses to lift them into place, then carved them off.

Boule: "Council"; the Athenian legislative body that formulated laws and state policy; *bouleutes:* a councillor.

bronze: A metal alloy composed of copper and tin.

capital: The decorative top piece of a column.

cella: The main room of a Greek temple, usually housing the cult image (statue) of the god to whom the temple was dedicated.

ceramos: Potter's clay.

choregus: A well-to-do backer of plays and other theatrical and cultural events.

colonnade: A row of columns.

cottabos: A party game in which drinkers tried to hit a target with the wine dregs left in their cups.

cuirass: A breastplate or other chest protection worn by an ancient infantryman.

decate: A postbirth ceremony in which parents named the newborn.

demes (demoi): Small geographical units or local communities in ancient Attica.

demos: The citizen body; or the sum of the state's democratic laws and institutions; or democrats; or the poorer citizens; or a local district (deme).

diaulos: A footrace of two *stades* (or about twelve hundred feet).

dicasts (dikastai): Jurors.

divination: The reading and interpretation of omens and other divine signs.

dokimasia: A rigid examination made of Athenian candidates for public office.

dolichos: A footrace of twenty to twenty-four *stades.*

drachma: A silver coin issued by Athens and some other Greek states. An Athenian drachma weighed 4.31 grams and was part of a system of currency in which 1 drachma=6 obols, 100 drachmas=1 mina, and 60 minae (6,000 drachmas)=1 talent. In the late fifth century B.C., the average Athenian worker and also a rower in the navy received a wage of 1 drachma per day; a juror received 3 obols (half a drachma) per day; a gallon of olive oil cost about 3 drachmas; a pair of shoes cost 6 to 8 drachmas; a slave cost 150 to 200 drachmas (or more if highly skilled); and land went for 200 to 300 drachmas per acre.

drum: A single cylindrical component of a column.

Ecclesia: The Athenian Assembly, or meeting of the citizens to elect leaders and discuss and vote on state policies.

ekechiria: The Olympic truce, during which Greek states were forbidden to make war or impose the death penalty.

engue: A formal betrothal, usually conducted in front of witnesses.

Epheboi: The Athenian military training corps; *ephebe* (plural, *epheboi*): a recruit in the corps; also used more generally to denote a young man between the ages of eighteen and twenty.

episkyros: A team ball game probably similar to modern rugby (which is itself a precursor of American football).

epitaphios: A funeral speech.

ergastirai: Athenian maidens who wove Athena's sacred robe.

freedman: A slave who gained his or her freedom.

frieze: A painted and/or sculpted ornamental band running around the perimeter of a building, most often a temple.

gamos: A wedding celebration.

genos: A clan, made up of several families.

grammatistes: Teachers of reading, writing, and simple mathematics.

greaves: Bronze shinguards worn by Greek hoplites.

gymnasium: A public facility in which men exercised, played sports, read, and attended lectures.

gymnastiki: "Exercise."

gymnos: "Naked."

gynaeceum (or *gynaikonitis*): The women's quarters of a Greek home.

Hades: The underworld; the realm of the afterlife.

Heraea: Women's athletic games held every four years in honor of the goddess Hera.

herm: A bust of the god Hermes placed near the front door of a house to ward off evil.

hetairai: "Companions"; high-class prostitutes; educated women who provided men with sex and intelligent conversation.

hoplite: A heavily armored infantry soldier.

hoplitodromos: A footrace in which the runners were fully or partially clad in armor.

hoplon (*aspis*): The shield carried by a hoplite.

isonomia: Equality under the law.

kalokagathia: A healthy balance between mental (or moral) and physical excellence.

kalos: "Beautiful."

kanephoroi: Young girls selected from aristocratic Athenian families to march in the Panathenaic procession.

kitharistes: Music teachers.

kubernetes: The helmsman on a Greek trireme, who was usually an experienced naval veteran.

kyrios: A woman's male guardian, usually her father or husband.

lekythus: A narrow-necked vase buried with the dead or left at the graveside.

linothorax: A cuirass made of layers of linen or canvas.

liturgies (*leitourgiai*): "The people's burdens"; financial support given by well-to-do individuals for producing plays, outfitting and maintaining warships, and other community services.

lochos: A small subdivision of the Greek phalanx composed of about one hundred men, though probably differing in size from one polis to another; *lochagos:* the officer in command of a *lochos.*

logographai: Professional speechwriters.

lyre (*lyra*): A small harp.

mercenary: A hired soldier.

metics (metoikoi): Foreigners (either Greeks from other city-states or non-Greeks) living in Athens.

moicheia: "Adultery."

mystery cult: A religious group whose initiations were kept secret.

obol: *See* drachma.

oikos: The family.

omen: A sign of impending good or bad fortune.

oracle: A message thought to come from the gods; or the sacred site where such a message was given; or the priestess who delivered the message.

ostracism: An Athenian democratic process in which the people voted to banish an unpopular leader; *ostrakon:* a pottery shard on which a citizen wrote the name of the person he wanted to see banished.

othismos: "The shoving"; a maneuver in which hoplites in the rear ranks of a phalanx pushed at their comrades' backs, forcefully thrusting the whole formation into the enemy's ranks; if the enemy was Greek, its phalanx pushed back.

ouragoi: "Rear rankers"; veteran officers who stood behind the phalanx and made sure the men in the rear ranks were doing their jobs.

paean: "Battle hymn"; a patriotic song sung by Greek hoplites as they marched into battle.

paidagogos: A slave or freedman who accompanied a boy to school and supervised his behavior there.

paidotribes: Athletics instructors.

palaestra: A wrestling school or facility, or a part of a gymnasium devoted to wrestling.

pale: "Wrestling."

panhellenic: "All-Greek."

pankration: A rough-and-tumble athletic event that combined elements of wrestling, boxing, and street fighting.

panoply: A hoplite's array of arms and armor.

parochos: At a wedding, the groom's best friend.

parrhesia: "Freedom of speech."

pediments: The triangular gables at the front and back of a classical temple.

peltasts (peltastai): Light-armed skirmishers, usually javelin men; *pelta:* the small round or crescent-shaped shield carried by a *peltast.*

peplos: Athena's sacred robe, a new version of which was presented to her during the Panathenaic festival.

periodos: "Circuit"; the "big four" athletic games of ancient Greece, including those held at Olympia, Isthmia, Delphi, and Nemea.

phalanx: A Greek military formation consisting of multiple ranks, with hoplites standing, marching, or fighting side by side in each rank.

phratry: "Blood brotherhood"; an extended kinship group composed of about thirty clans.

phyle: A tribe, usually composed of three phratries; *phylarch:* a tribal leader.

point: A common sculptor's tool.

polis: In Greece, a city-state, or tiny nation built around a central town or city.

polluted: Religiously unclean or tainted.

porpax: A bronze loop on the back of a hoplite's shield through which he placed his left arm.

probouleumata: Legislative bills formulated in the Boule dealing with state business and community affairs.

psyche: The soul.

pteruges: "Feathers"; strips of linen, canvas, or leather comprising the bottom part of a hoplite's linen cuirass.

pyre (pyra): A pile of wood on which a body was cremated.

sanctuary: A sacred area made up of a temple and its surrounding grounds.

sitesis: The state's granting of free meals to athletes who won at the circuit games.

skene: "Scene building"; a structure facing the audience area in a theater and containing dressing rooms for the actors.

sphairai: Balls.

stade: A footrace of about six hundred feet.

stoa: A roofed public building, usually long with an open colonnade along one side.

Strategia: Athens's board of ten generals; *strategos* (plural, *strategoi*): a general, an office annually elected by the Assembly.

symposium: A dinner party, usually in a private home.

taxeis: Large subdivisions of the Athenian phalanx, of which there were ten in all, each drawn from one of the city's tribes; *taxiarchos:* the officer in command of one of the *taxeis*.

telesterion: The initiation hall of a mystery cult.

terra-cotta: Baked clay.

tethrippon: A long race for four-horse chariots.

thallophoroi: "Bearers of green branches"; elderly Athenian men who marched in the Panathenaic procession.

theatron: The audience area of a theater.

thetes: Members of Athens's poorer classes.

thymele: The altar in a Greek theater.

trierarch (trierarchos): The captain of a trireme; in Athens during the Classic Age, a trierarch assumed such command as part of a public duty, a liturgy known as the Trierarchy.

trireme: An ancient warship with three banks of oars, the *thranite* (upper), *zygite* (middle), and *thalamite* (lower).

trophy (tropaion): A wooden framework displaying captured enemy arms and armor, set up on the battlefield to celebrate victory and give thanks to the gods.

For Further Reading

Isaac Asimov, *The Greeks: A Great Adventure*. Boston: Houghton Mifflin, 1965. An excellent, entertaining overview of Greek history and culture.

David Bellingham, *An Introduction to Greek Mythology*. Secaucus, NJ: Chartwell Books, 1989. Explains the major Greek myths and legends and their importance to the ancient Greeks. Contains many beautiful photos and drawings.

C. M. Bowra, *Classical Greece*. New York: Time-Life, 1965. Despite the passage of more than thirty years, this volume, written by a renowned classical historian and adorned with numerous maps, drawings, and color photos, is only slightly dated and remains one of the best introductions to ancient Greece for general readers.

Peter Connolly, *The Greek Armies*. Morristown, NJ: Silver Burdette, 1979. A fine, detailed study of Greek armor, weapons, and battle tactics, filled with colorful, accurate illustrations by Connolly, the world's leading artistic interpreter of the ancient world. Highly recommended.

Denise Dersin, *Greece: Temples, Tombs, and Treasures*. Alexandria, VA: Time-Life Books, 1994. In a way a newer companion volume to Bowra's book (see above), this is also excellent and features a long, up-to-date, and beautifully illustrated chapter on Athens's golden age.

Rhoda A. Hendricks, ed. and trans., *Classical Gods and Heroes: Myths as Told by the Ancient Authors*. New York: Morrow Quill, 1974. A collection of easy-to-read translations of famous Greek myths and tales as told by ancient Greek and Roman writers, including Homer, Hesiod, Pindar, Apollodorus, Ovid, and Virgil.

Susan Peach and Anne Millard, *The Greeks*. London: Usborne, 1990. A general overview of the history, culture, myths, and everyday life of ancient Greece, presented in a format suitable to young readers (although the many fine, accurate color illustrations make the book appealing to anyone interested in ancient Greece).

Jonathon Rutland, *See Inside an Ancient Greek Town*. New York: Barnes and Noble, 1995. This colorful introduction to ancient Greek life is aimed at basic readers.

John Warry, *Warfare in the Classical World*. Norman: University of Oklahoma Press, 1995. A beautifully mounted book filled with accurate and useful paintings, drawings, maps, and diagrams. The text is also first rate, providing much detailed information about the weapons, clothing, strategies, battle tactics, and military leaders of the Greeks, Romans, and the peoples they fought.

Author's Note: In the following volumes, I provide much useful background information about Greek history and culture, including the Greek-Persian conflict; the rise and fall of the Athenian empire; the golden age of arts, literature, and architecture; and sketches of the important Greek politicians, military leaders, writers, and artists. Though they are aimed at high school readers, the high level of detail and documentation in these volumes make them useful for older general readers as well.

Don Nardo, *Greek and Roman Theater.* San Diego: Lucent Books, 1995.

———, *The Battle of Marathon.* San Diego: Lucent Books, 1996.

———, *The Age of Pericles.* San Diego: Lucent Books, 1996.

———, *Life in Ancient Greece.* San Diego: Lucent Books, 1996.

———, *The Trial of Socrates.* San Diego: Lucent Books, 1997.

———, *Scientists of Ancient Greece.* San Diego: Lucent Books, 1998.

———, *The Parthenon.* San Diego: Lucent Books, 1999.

———, *Greek and Roman Sport.* San Diego: Lucent Books, 1999.

———, *Leaders of Ancient Greece.* San Diego: Lucent Books, 1999.

Works Consulted

Ancient Sources

Aeschylus, *The Persians,* in *Aeschylus: Prometheus Bound, the Suppliants, Seven Against Thebes, the Persians.* Trans. Philip Vellacott. Baltimore: Penguin Books, 1961; and the *Oresteia,* published as *The Orestes Plays of Aeschylus.* Trans. Paul Roche. New York: New American Library, 1962.

Aristotle, *The Athenian Constitution.* Trans. H. Rackham. 1952. Reprint, Cambridge, MA: Harvard University Press, 1996.

Kenneth J. Atchity, ed., *The Classical Greek Reader.* New York: Oxford University Press, 1996. A collection of translations of ancient Greek writings, including those of Homer, Solon, Herodotus, Lysias, Xenophon, Aristotle, Sophocles, Demosthenes, and many others.

Epictetus, *Discourses.* Trans. W. A. Oldfather. 2 vols. Cambridge, MA: Harvard University Press, 1995.

Moses Hadas, ed., *The Complete Plays of Aristophanes.* New York: Bantam Books, 1962.

Herodotus, *The Histories.* Trans. Aubrey de Sélincourt. New York: Penguin Books, 1972.

Cornelius Nepos, *The Book of the Great Generals of Foreign Nations.* Trans. John Rolfe. Cambridge, MA: Harvard University Press, 1960.

Pausanias, *Guide to Greece.* Trans. Peter Levi. 2 vols. New York: Penguin Books, 1971.

Pindar, *The Odes of Pindar.* Trans. C. M. Bowra. New York: Penguin Books, 1969.

Plato, *Dialogues,* in *The Dialogues of Plato.* Trans. Benjamin Jowett. Chicago: Encyclopaedia Britannica, 1952.

Plutarch, *Parallel Lives,* excerpted in *The Rise and Fall of Athens: Nine Greek Lives by Plutarch.* Trans. Ian Scott-Kilvert. New York: Penguin, 1960.

J. J. Pollitt, ed. and trans., *The Art of Ancient Greece: Sources and Documents.* New York: Cambridge University Press, 1990. A compilation of translations of ancient sources dealing with painting, sculpture, architecture, and other artistic genres.

Polybius, *Histories,* published as *Polybius: The Rise of the Roman Empire.* Trans. Ian Scott-Kilvert. New York: Penguin Books, 1979.

Sophocles, *Electra and Other Plays.* Trans. E. F. Watling. Baltimore: Penguin Books, 1953.

Waldo E. Sweet, ed., *Sport and Recreation in Ancient Greece: A Sourcebook with Translations.* New York: Oxford University Press, 1987. A collection of translations of ancient sources describing sports, games, music, dance, theater, and related leisure activities.

Theophrastus, *Characters.* Trans. Jeffrey Rustin. Cambridge, MA: Harvard University Press, 1993.

Thucydides, *The Peloponnesian War.* Trans. Rex Warner. New York: Penguin Books, 1972; and also published as *The Landmark Thucydides: A Comprehensive Guide to the Peloponnesian War.* Trans. Richard Crawley, ed. Robert B. Strassler. New York: Simon and Schuster, 1996.

Vitruvius, *On Architecture.* Trans. Frank Granger. 2 vols. Cambridge, MA: Harvard University Press, 1962.

Thomas Wiedemann, ed., *Greek and Roman Slavery.* Baltimore: Johns Hopkins University Press, 1981. A compilation of translations of ancient sources dealing with slavery.

Xenophon, *Anabasis*. Trans. W. H. D. Rouse. New York: New American Library, 1959.

———, *Hellenica*, published as *A History of My Times*. Trans. Rex Warner. New York: Penguin Books, 1979.

———, *Memorabilia and Oeconomicus*. Trans. E. C. Marchant. Cambridge, MA: Harvard University Press, 1965.

———, *Scripta Minora*. Trans. E. C. Marchant. Cambridge, MA: Harvard University Press, 1993.

Modern Sources

Architecture, Engineering, and Acropolis Complex

Bruce Allsopp, *A History of Classical Architecture*. London: Sir Isaac Pitman and Sons, 1965.

Manolis Andronicos, *The Acropolis*. Athens: Ekdotike Athenon, 1994.

John Boardman, *The Parthenon and Its Sculptures*. Austin: University of Texas Press, 1985.

Vincent J. Bruno, ed., *The Parthenon*. New York: Norton, 1974.

L. Sprague de Camp, *The Ancient Engineers*. New York: Ballantine Books, 1963.

Peter Green, *The Parthenon*. New York: Newsweek Book Division, 1973.

Ian Jenkins, *The Parthenon Frieze*. Austin: University of Texas Press, 1994.

A. W. Lawrence, *Greek Architecture*. Rev. R. A. Tomlinson. New Haven, CT: Yale University Press, 1996.

John Miliadis, *The Acropolis*. Athens: M. Pechlivanidis, n.d.

Panayotis Tournikiotis, ed., *The Parthenon and Its Impact in Modern Times*. New York: Harry N. Abrams, 1996.

R. E. Wycherly, *The Stones of Athens*. Princeton, NJ: Princeton University Press, 1978.

Art and Sculpture

Carl Bluemel, *Greek Sculptors at Work*. London: Phaidon, 1969.

John Boardman, *Greek Art*. New York: Praeger, 1964.

———, ed., *The Oxford History of Classical Art*. Oxford: Oxford University Press, 1993.

Thomas Craven, *The Pocket Book of Greek Art*. New York: Pocket Books, 1950.

G. M. A. Richter, *Portraits of the Greeks*. Rev. R. R. R. Smith. Ithaca, NY: Cornell University Press, 1984.

Nigel Spivey, *Greek Art*. London: Phaidon, 1997.

Gods, Myths, Worship, Burial Customs, and Religious Festivals

Walter Burkert, *Greek Religion, Archaic and Classical*. Oxford: Basil Blackwell, 1985.

Robert Garland, *The Greek Way of Death*. Ithaca, NY: Cornell University Press, 1985.

Michael Grant, *Myths of the Greeks and Romans*. New York: Penguin Books, 1962.

Evi Melas, *Temples and Sanctuaries of Ancient Greece*. London: Thames and Hudson, 1973.

Jon D. Mikalson, *Athenian Popular Religion*. Chapel Hill: University of North Carolina Press, 1983.

Mark P. O. Morford and Robert J. Lenardon, *Classical Mythology*. New York: Longman, 1985.

Jennifer Neils, *Goddess and Polis: The Panathenaic Festival in Ancient Athens*. Princeton, NJ: Princeton University Press, 1992.

———, ed., *Worshipping Athena: Panathenaia and Parthenon*. Madison: University of Wisconsin Press, 1996. (*Note:* The author's spelling of the great Athenian festival is an acceptable variant of Panathenaea.)

Erika Simon, *Festivals of Attica: An Archaeological Commentary.* Madison: University of Wisconsin Press, 1983.

Literature, Theater, Philosophy, and Ideas

H. C. Baldry, *The Greek Tragic Theater.* New York: W. W. Norton, 1971.

C. M. Bowra, *Homer.* New York: Scribner's, 1972.

James H. Butler, *The Theater and Drama of Greece and Rome.* San Francisco: Chandler, 1972.

Lionel Casson, *Masters of Ancient Comedy.* New York: Macmillan, 1960.

E. R. Dodds, *The Greeks and the Irrational.* Berkeley and Los Angeles: University of California Press, 1968.

Michael Grant, *Greek and Roman Historians: Information and Misinformation.* London: Routledge, 1995.

Victor D. Hanson and John Heath, *Who Killed Homer?: The Demise of Classical Education and the Recovery of Greek Wisdom.* New York: Free Press, 1998.

Bernard M. W. Knox, *The Heroic Temper: Studies in Sophoclean Tragedy.* Berkeley and Los Angeles: University of California Press, 1966.

Peter Levi, *A History of Greek Literature.* New York: Viking, 1985.

Don Nardo, ed., *Readings on Sophocles.* San Diego: Greenhaven Press, 1997.

——, *Readings on Homer.* San Diego: Greenhaven Press, 1998.

Aubrey de Sélincourt, *The World of Herodotus.* San Francisco: North Point Press, 1982.

Rex Warner, *The Greek Philosophers.* New York: New American Library, 1958.

Politics, Democracy, Citizenship, and Legal Institutions

David Cohen, *Law, Violence, and Community in Classical Athens.* New York: Cambridge University Press, 1995.

J. K. Davies, *Democracy and Classical Greece.* Cambridge, MA: Harvard University Press, 1993.

W. G. Forrest, *The Emergence of Greek Democracy.* New York: World University Library, 1966.

Kathleen Freeman, *The Murder of Herodes and Other Trials from the Athenian Law Courts.* New York: W. W. Norton, 1963.

A. H. M. Jones, *Athenian Democracy.* 1957. Reprint, Baltimore: Johns Hopkins University Press, 1995.

Douglas M. MacDowell, *The Law in Classical Athens.* Ithaca, NY: Cornell University Press, 1978.

Eli Sagan, *The Honey and the Hemlock: Democracy and Paranoia in Ancient Athens and Modern America.* New York: HarperCollins, 1991.

Alfred Zimmern, *The Greek Commonwealth: Politics and Economics in Fifth-Century Athens.* Rev. ed. New York: Oxford University Press, 1961.

Social Institutions and Customs

Sue Blundell, *Women in Ancient Greece.* Cambridge, MA: Harvard University Press, 1995.

James Davidson, *Courtesans and Fishcakes: The Consuming Passions of Classical Athens.* New York: St. Martin's Press, 1998.

Victor Ehrenberg, *The People of Aristophanes: A Sociology of Old Attic Comedy.* New York: Schocken Books, 1962.

N. R. E. Fisher, *Social Values in Classical Athens.* London: Dent, 1976.

Robert Garland, *The Greek Way of Life.* Ithaca, NY: Cornell University Press, 1990.

Mark Golden, *Children and Childhood in Classical Athens.* Baltimore: Johns Hopkins University Press, 1990.

Eva C. Keuls, *The Reign of the Phallus: Sexual Politics in Ancient Athens.* New York: Harper and Row, 1985.

Sarah B. Pomeroy, *Goddesses, Whores, Wives, and Slaves: Women in Classical Antiquity.* New York: Schocken Books, 1995.

Sports and Games

M. I. Finley and H. W. Pleket, *The Olympic Games: The First Thousand Years.* New York: Viking Press, 1976.

Vera Olivova, *Sports and Games in the Ancient World.* New York: St. Martin's Press, 1984.

David Sansone, *Greek Athletics and the Genesis of Sport.* Berkeley and Los Angeles: University of California Press, 1988.

Judith Swaddling, *The Ancient Olympic Games.* Austin: University of Texas Press, 1996.

D. C. Young, *The Olympic Myth of Greek Amateur Athletics.* Chicago: Ares, 1984.

Studies of Prominent Ancient Athenian Figures

J. K. Anderson, *Xenophon.* New York: Scribner's, 1974.

Jonathon Barnes, *Aristotle.* New York: Oxford University Press, 1982.

Walter M. Ellis, *Alcibiades.* New York: Routledge, 1989.

J. A. S. Evans, *Herodotus.* Boston: Twayne, 1982.

Kathleen Freeman, *The Work and Life of Solon, with a Translation of His Poems.* 1926. Reprint, New York: Arno, 1976.

Michael Grant, *The Classical Greeks.* New York: Scribner's, 1989.

R. M. Hare, *Plato.* New York: Oxford University Press, 1982.

Simon Hornblower, *Thucydides.* Baltimore: Johns Hopkins University Press, 1987.

Werner Jaeger, *Demosthenes.* Berkeley and Los Angeles: University of California Press, 1938.

Donald Kagan, *Pericles of Athens and the Birth of Democracy.* New York: Free Press, 1991.

Robert B. Kebric, *Greek People.* Mountain View, CA: Mayfield, 1997.

A. J. Podlecki, *The Life of Themistocles.* Montreal: McGill-Queen's University Press, 1975.

A. E. Taylor, *Socrates: The Man and His Thought.* New York: Doubleday, 1952.

War, Weapons, and Military Customs and Tactics

F. E. Adcock, *The Greek and Macedonian Art of War.* Berkeley and Los Angeles: University of California Press, 1957.

J. K. Anderson, *Military Theory and Practice in the Age of Xenophon.* Berkeley and Los Angeles: University of California Press, 1970.

Andrew R. Burn, *Persia and the Greeks: The Defense of the West, c. 546–478 B.C.* London: Edward Arnold, 1962.

Peter Connolly, *Greece and Rome at War.* London: Greenhill Books, 1998.

Peter Green, *The Greco-Persian Wars.* Berkeley and Los Angeles: University of California Press, 1996.

John Hackett, ed., *Warfare in the Ancient World.* New York: Facts On File, 1989.

Victor D. Hanson, *The Western Way of War: Infantry Battle in Classical Greece.* New York: Oxford University Press, 1989.

Donald Kagan, *The Outbreak of the Peloponnesian War.* Ithaca, NY: Cornell University Press, 1969.

John Lazenby, *The Defense of Greece.* Bloomington, IL: David Brown, 1993.

A. M. Snodgrass, *Arms and Armour of the Greeks.* Ithaca, NY: Cornell University Press, 1967.

General Studies of Ancient Athens at Its Height

C. M. Bowra, *Periclean Athens.* New York: Dial Press, 1971.

Joint Association of Classical Teachers, *The World of Athens: An Introduction to Classical Athenian Culture.* New York: Cambridge University Press, 1984.

Malcolm F. McGregor, *The Athenians and Their Empire.* Vancouver: University of British Columbia Press, 1987.

Christian Meier, *Athens: Portrait of a City in Its Golden Age.* Trans. Robert and Rita Kimber. New York: Henry Holt, 1998.

Russell Meiggs, *The Athenian Empire.* Oxford: Clarendon Press, 1972.

C. A. Robinson, *Athens in the Age of Pericles.* Norman: University of Oklahoma, 1971.

George D. Wilcoxon, *Athens Ascendant.* Ames: Iowa State University Press, 1979.

General Ancient Greek History, Geography, and Culture

Lesly Adkins and Roy A. Adkins, *Handbook to Life in Ancient Greece.* New York: Facts On File, 1997.

C. M. Bowra, *The Greek Experience.* New York: New American Library, 1957.

Andrew R. Burn, *The Penguin History of Greece.* New York: Penguin Books, 1985.

J. B. Bury, *A History of Greece to the Death of Alexander.* Rev. Russell Meiggs. London: Macmillan, 1975.

John A. Crow, *Greece: The Magic Spring.* New York: Harper and Row, 1970.

Victor Ehrenberg, *From Solon to Socrates: Greek History and Civilization During the Sixth and Fifth Centuries B.C.* London: Methuen, 1967.

M. I. Finley, *The Ancient Greeks: An Introduction to Their Life and Thought.* New York: Viking Press, 1964.

Michael Grant, *The Rise of the Greeks.* New York: Macmillan, 1987.

———, *A Guide to the Ancient World.* New York: Barnes and Noble, 1996.

Ian Jenkins, *Greek and Roman Life.* Cambridge, MA: Harvard University Press, 1986.

Peter Levi, *Atlas of the Greek World.* New York: Facts On File, 1984.

Thomas R. Martin, *Ancient Greece: From Prehistoric to Hellenistic Times.* New Haven, CT: Yale University Press, 1996.

C. E. Robinson, *Everyday Life in Ancient Greece.* Oxford: Clarendon Press, 1968.

Chester G. Starr, *A History of the Ancient World.* New York: Oxford University Press, 1991.

Richard J. A. Talbert, ed., *Atlas of Classical History.* London: Routledge, 1985.

Index

Picture Credits

About the Author

Classical historian and award-winning writer Don Nardo has published more than thirty books about the ancient Greek and Roman world. These include general histories such as *The Roman Empire, The Persian Empire,* and *The Age of Pericles;* cultural studies such as *Greek and Roman Theater, The Parthenon, Life of a Roman Slave,* and *Scientists of Ancient Greece;* biographies of Julius Caesar and Cleopatra; and literary companions to the works of Homer and Sophocles. Mr. Nardo also writes screenplays and teleplays and composes music. He lives with his lovely wife, Christine, and dog, Bud, on Cape Cod, Massachusetts.